Praise for
The Single Dad's Survival Guide

"This is the most informative and genuinely helpful guide for single fathers that I've read in my twenty-seven years of divorce recovery work. Mike Klumpp covers all the bases. His honest presentation will help any single dad navigate the wilderness of single parenting."

—JIM SMOKE, speaker and author of the bestseller *Growing Through Divorce*

"*The Single Dad's Survival Guide* is filled with flashes of brilliant practical insight born of learning the hard way. I'll be recommending this book to the thousands of single fathers that I share with yearly."

—GARY RICHMOND, pastor to single parents at First Evangelical Free Church of Fullerton, California, and author of *Successful Single Parenting*

"My most frustrating cases in counseling are single fathers who suddenly have custody of their children. *The Single Dad's Survival Guide* is a valuable tool to minister to this unique group of men. After reviewing this book, I immediately sent it to a new single father of two children."

—DR. JIM A. TALLEY, www.drtalley.com, counselor and author of *Reconcilable Differences* and *Too Close Too Soon*

"For a single dad, it doesn't have to be pretty—it just has to work. Mike Klumpp plunges in and stirs things up, offering honest, straightforward help. Bottom line: Read this book."

—BILL BUTTERWORTH, speaker, author of *When Life Doesn't Turn Out Like You Planned,* and coauthor of *The Promise of the Second Wind*

"Mike Klumpp challenges fathers with humor, support, and insight into the thankless job of single parenting. His humbling honesty provides the friendly groundwork for practical suggestions and clarifying questions. From Romans 8:37 to recipes, rebellious teens to respectful transitions, Mike claims his faith and fatherhood—inviting others to join him."

—TINA MOODY, M.DIV., M.A., L.P.C., theologian and psychotherapist

"Single dads don't experience *Leave It to Beaver;* they live in *Apocalypse Now.* Mike Klumpp is determined to honestly pass along his hard-won insights and skills to all fathers who really want to get better at fatherhood. I wish this book had been around when my kids were young."

—BOB BENNETT, songwriter and recording artist whose *Songs from Bright Avenue* album deals with divorce recovery

"From the first page of *The Single Dad's Survival Guide,* you enter the no-fluff zone of practical tools that will not only get you through today but will provide a guide for many days to come. Feeling lonely, angry, in need of a twenty-seven-hour day? Mike Klumpp will help."

—REG GRANT, professor at Dallas Theological Seminary and author of *Storm, the Surprising Story of Martin Luther*

"This is a warm and helpful resource for confused hearts. Alternately funny and heartbreaking, *The Single Dad's Survival Guide* is practical encouragement served up with a kick!"

—LEN WOODS, pastor and author of *Praying God's Promises in Tough Times*

"Rooted in Mike's pain and perseverance, this book is as straightforward and practical a guide as you'll find on effective fatherhood. While the book targets single dads, I found it to be inspiring and instructive on fatherhood in general. It gave me renewed vision for being a 'real man' for my wife and children."

—MO LEVERETT, recording artist, and founder and director of Desire Street Ministries in New Orleans

THE

Single Dad's
SURVIVAL
GUIDE

How to Succeed
As a One-Man
Parenting Team

THE

Single Dad's

SURVIVAL

GUIDE

MIKE KLUMPP

WATERBROOK
PRESS

THE SINGLE DAD'S SURVIVAL GUIDE
PUBLISHED BY WATERBROOK PRESS
2375 Telstar Drive, Suite 160
Colorado Springs, Colorado 80920
A division of Random House, Inc.

All Scripture quotations, unless otherwise indicated, are taken from the *Holy Bible, New International Version*®. NIV®. Copyright © 1973, 1978, 1984 by International Bible Society. Used by permission of Zondervan Publishing House. All rights reserved. Scripture quotations marked (NASB) are taken from the *New American Standard Bible*®. © Copyright The Lockman Foundation 1960, 1962, 1963, 1968, 1971, 1972, 1973, 1975, 1977, 1995. Used by permission. (www.Lockman.org).

Italics in Scripture quotations reflect the author's added emphasis.

The author has made every effort to ensure the truthfulness of the stories and anecdotes in this book. In a few instances, names and identifying details have been changed to protect the privacy of the persons involved.

ISBN 1-57856-670-3

Library of Congress Cataloging-in-Publication Data

Klumpp, Mike.
    The single dad's survival guide : how to succeed as a one-man parenting team /
by Mike Klumpp.— 1st ed.
        p. cm.
    ISBN 1-57856-670-3
    1. Parenting—Religious aspects—Christianity. 2. Single fathers—Religious life. I. Title.
    BV4529.K59 2003
    248.8'421—dc21

                                                                        2003010007

Printed in the United States of America
2003—First Edition

10 9 8 7 6 5 4 3 2 1

To Jennifer, Ian, Paige, and Nico,
the four best guinea pigs on God's green earth.

I love you,
Dad

CONTENTS

Chapter 6

Chapter 7

Chapter 8

Chapter 9

Chapter 10

ACKNOWLEDGMENTS

To Margaret, John, Frank, Rick, Mike, Josie, and others: Thanks.

To all the single parents who helped by sharing their own hard-won success stories: Many thanks for making this book possible and for multiplying the impact of your wisdom to untold numbers of other single parents.

To all single parents reading this book: The cavalry is on the way. Hang in there.

To my gracious Father: Thank you for the challenges that have made me a stronger warrior and a better man. And thank you for the gift of your Son.

A special thanks to Karen: Without you none of this would be possible. Thanks for being a special friend and soul mate.

THIS JOB CALLS FOR A MAN

Single Parenting Takes All You've Got, So Give It Your All

THIS IS A BOOK for men who are well acquainted with the words *difficult, exhausting,* and *frustrating.* Like you, I'm an expert at running into the wall, falling down, then getting up and running into the wall again. The challenges of being a single dad are not mastered in a few months or even a few years. It's an ongoing learning process. But we can gain new insight and learn core skills, and together we can overcome the biggest hurdles and become the dads our kids so desperately need.

Whether we are our children's primary caregiver, like myself; whether we are single because we lost our spouse, like my friend Frank; or whether we are giving care and guidance to our kids mostly on weekends, like my buddy Ron, we need honest solutions to the problems we keep butting into. And we need *real* help to get us through today.

So let's be honest. We can admit we're angry and bitter and hurting. We can drop our defenses and acknowledge that everything's *not* all right and that we wonder if it ever will be. We can fess up to our doubts—and even fears—about the future. All of this uncertainty is understandable, since we're engaged in something that's nowhere near as easy as changing careers and landing a new job or even surviving boot camp. This is a huge challenge and one that we really need to succeed at, but how in heaven's name can we do it?

Let's begin by being open about our anxieties and worries and confronting the Big Questions that keep us awake at night: *How can I be the dad my kids need right now? How can I help them through the hurt when I feel suffocated by pain myself? And how can I do all of this alone?*

I've asked those questions hundreds of times over the past few years.[1] I haven't found all the answers, to be sure, but I've found enough solutions to make the task of single fatherhood a doable, satisfying, even successful enterprise. And it all begins with something really simple: being a man.

God intended for kids to be raised by two people, a man and a woman. When you're working with a partner as a team, parenting can be a wonderful task. Like WWF tag-team wrestling, when one of you gets tired, *tag,* just send in the fresh parent.

But once you're divorced, separated, or widowed, you're no longer half of a team. You're alone. Whether you have your kids every weekend, one week a month, full time, or at Christmas and during summer vacations, you know they're looking to you for certain things. And you want with all your heart to provide what they need.

But how?

BE A MAN ABOUT IT

This book talks about a lot of things, but the advice pretty much boils down to doing one thing well—*you've got to be a man.* Specifically, you've got to be the man your kids need. I write as a Christian, so my understanding of manhood is colored by Christian teaching on God and humanity. I believe God created men with special abilities: strength, leadership, discipline, vision, and organization, among others. We all reflect these qualities in varying degrees and combinations. But men also are designed to provide security, solidity, confidence, and safety for their kids. Yes, we have to work hard at it to do it well, but the basics are already there.

Men also are capable of responding to their kids' other essential needs: to be loved, to be nurtured, to be listened to, to be patiently cared for, and to be understood. These may not come as naturally to the typical American male, but they are still possible. With God's help we can nurture as well as discipline. We can be tender and loving while providing strength. We can patiently listen to our kids and work overtime to understand them, all while establishing leadership and vision.

Thank God that you're a man and that he has placed you in a position to help your kids through the present crisis. Thank him for giving you this challenging opportunity to raise your children to become well balanced, productive, emotionally and spiritually healthy adults. We all know it's not simple, but it *is* possible. In the chapters that follow, I'll share strategies and practical tips—many of them learned by trial and error—that will point you in the direction of success.

WHY I HAD TO WRITE THIS BOOK

Not long after my divorce, one of my daughters had a crisis that is uniquely a girl issue. I don't care how much guys think they know, there are still areas of life that, for a girl, really call for a woman's involvement. My ex-wife was living in another city, and I didn't even have her daytime telephone number. So I did something that's hard for a lot of guys to do: I asked for help. I called some neighborhood moms for advice, then I dashed off to the local bookstore. After searching the shelves for a good book on single parenting, I finally asked my friend who ran the store for a recommendation. She laughed and told me there were few books on single parenting, and even fewer from a Christian worldview.

"Someone needs to write one," I said.

"You do it!" she laughed.

I remember thinking, *Yeah, what single dad has time to write a book?* However, several years and many discussions with struggling single parents later, I decided to *make* the time.

By the way, the phrase *struggling single parent* is sort of like saying *dysfunctional family.* It's redundant. And it's a given. Single parents struggle. Period. But now that you find yourself raising your children by yourself, don't lose hope. Remember, we're doing this together.

A BLACK BELT IN PARENTING?

For close to thirty years I've been practicing backfists and front kicks as a martial artist. These moves are fundamental to good karate. Having repeated them over and over for almost three decades, I'm beginning to do them well.

I find that the same principles apply to single parenting. Over the years, with practice—and lots of repetition—I have learned to do some things pretty well. At first I tried (and failed) at a lot of things, but in most cases I learned from my mistakes and found workable and at times surprising solutions. This book will focus on these solutions. While your particular circumstances are different from mine, I'm confident you'll find plenty here to help lighten the load, give you hope, and set you and your kids on a path to greater love and healing and a confident future. Pay particular attention to the practical, hands-on helps at the end of each chapter. These will encourage and direct you in accomplishing important goals. Use the strategies in this book as a starting point to develop your own solutions, tailored to your unique situation and your children's needs. This book is not a set of rules but a foundation for building a home with your kids, who are looking to you right now to be the anchor they need.

I'm not writing as an "expert." I don't have a degree in psychology or social work. I'm not a counselor. But I served for years as a pastor and a chaplain. And I approach life with a burning desire to help others in their struggles, just as so many have helped me. I also write as a concerned single dad and a man who has benefited from a wide range of life experiences—from martial-arts instructor to football coach to weatherman actor and playwright to theater director to carpet salesman.

But the main reason I want to help other single dads is deeply spiritual: God has freely given his grace to me as a parent. He has loved and nurtured me through this whole ordeal. In the same way, I want to pass on some of God's goodness to you. I want to provide for you what I wish had been available to me several years ago. I want to give you a shoulder to cry on and a supportive voice to encourage you throughout the process.

Together we are serving our families in one of the most difficult tasks a man can undertake. May this book serve to lighten the burden and further prepare us all to raise healthy, confident children.

Landing on Your Feet

And Learning to Move Forward

My wife left me on a Saturday afternoon.

Three of our children were at a friend's house for swimming and a barbecue; my wife was out with our youngest child. She pulled up to the friend's house, dropped off the child, and left for a fresh start in another city miles away.

I had known there was trouble, but now I knew for certain that it was all over. Our marriage, our family, everything we worked for.

The next day I was supposed to host a party for the cast and crew of a play I had directed at the local opera house. Dozens of people were coming over at six that evening.

Was this a joke? My wife just left me, and I'm supposed to *have a party?*

Caught Off Guard

Single parenting usually catches us completely off guard no matter how many months (or even years) we've seen it coming. We start out happily married only to suddenly find ourselves divorced.

I say "find ourselves divorced" because for those of us who are committed to the institution of marriage, we never thought of divorce as a possibility. And yet we wake up one day and find it has happened. But until the moment that all the divorce papers are signed and the decree is issued, we live with the hope that *something* will happen to turn the tide and repair our marriage. Now that hope has died.[1]

I remember a friend telling me that even during the court battle over custody of his kids, he believed his wife would suddenly realize this was the wrong thing to do to their family. He believed they would reconcile right there in the courtroom and walk away to repair their relationship and live happily ever after.

I know what he's saying. Even though my own marriage had been in trouble for a while, I kept waiting for a miracle. I had prayed my heart out, believing that God would honor my requests that he keep my family intact. I couldn't believe that God would allow my marriage to fail when I was so willing to do whatever it took to make it work. But things fell apart anyway. Months later I got a call from my attorney and went in to pick up the final decree. I was stunned. Hope finally died.

Along with the death of hope come anger, hurt, and grief. You know the feelings. Perhaps we began the grieving process long ago, before the official legal process was ever launched. But until it was a finality, at least we had the fallback position of denial. Even though everything was falling apart, we could still somehow pretend it wasn't unraveling. We could cling to the thin hope that *something* would happen to turn things around. But divorce happened anyway. It happens every day, even to good people.

My marriage had been ending for some time. But not until that Saturday afternoon, when my wife left our youngest child behind and drove away in a fully packed van, did it really hit me. No amount of advance warning could have prepared me for the devastating emotions. I suddenly found myself alone with four children to raise.

For sixteen years I had believed in the solemn, lifelong vow that my wife and I took on our wedding day. We both had our problems and we both made mistakes. However, I felt we could make it through anything. I was wrong. We were defeated by anger.

I was angry over childhood issues that kept resurfacing. My wife was angry with me for not meeting her needs. I was supposed to be her protector, but anger had made me an enemy instead. Neither of us took our anger to God for healing. Instead, we acted out our anger in hurtful ways that deep-sixed our marriage. We were capable of inflicting pain through anger and in a multitude of other ways. We violated the trust we had placed in each other to the extent that solemn vows became irreparably broken.

My wife and I had stopped talking, except for brief phone calls, several months earlier. She had moved into an apartment while we tried to work things out. We attempted counseling (three different counselors) and psychologists, but our trust and communication were so diminished that there was nowhere to lay a new foundation to build on. Attempts to come close in intimacy brought greater anger and pain. There was fear of manipulation. For every step we took toward trying to heal our marriage, we seemed to take two steps back. We felt we were locked in our pain, with no possible way to escape the suffering.

After months of counseling, fighting, warming up, and then freezing out again, our marriage collapsed. My wife felt she needed distance, so she moved to a different city to make a new beginning and try to find her life again. She left the children with me, sensing that this would hurt the kids less than it would if she were to uproot them and further disrupt their lives.

The emotional upheaval threw me off my feet. I felt defeated, forgotten, abandoned by my wife, my God, and my world. It was one day after she left, and I was a wreck. How in the world could I throw a party?

Adjusting to the New Reality

I awoke that morning feeling numb. But the world kept turning with absolutely no concern for my woes. I needed to get supplies for the cast party, but I couldn't focus. I have a strong will, but I couldn't force my mind away from the pain.

This is when I began to learn a principle that helped get me through: I didn't have to face life entirely alone. In this case, a friend volunteered to help me buy food and supplies for the party. I pushed the cart along in a daze while my friend selected the items needed for that evening.

I felt I had to make sure the party was a success, both as part of my job as theater director and for my own sake. It was necessary for my self-image and to let my employers know I could still do the job. My friend helped me get the house ready and set the tables, and she was a quiet hostess for me. I was only there in body and false smile. Her simple act of friendship has forever indebted me to this caring, generous friend.

When my wife left, and later when the divorce became final, my life could easily have spun out of control. I couldn't escape the relentless urge to react to my pain by punishing my wife, by screaming to the heavens that this was the epitome of injustice, to punch a hole in the wall. I felt I needed to do *something* to rid myself of the pent-up rage and hurt. But instead, I fought to keep control.

Then there was the temptation to numb the pain with women, food, alcohol, and staying out late with friends. I felt an urgency to prove to myself and others that I was still the man I used to be. I wanted to prove I was desirable and that I wasn't a bad person.

My friend Rick, who shares custody of his children with his ex, confronted the same struggle. "At first there was a lot of anger, a lot of hate," he says. "Then there was alcohol abuse. Then I realized I needed to compensate for the loss of income, so I found more work. I started working eighteen to twenty hours a day, five and six days a week. Anything to keep my mind off my problems."

Ron, a friend with weekend-only custody, described his pain with the word *silence.*

"I was just so painfully lonely," he recalls. "There was no one with me. Where there had been music, television, laughter, and voices, there was just silence. It was a constant reminder of being alone. Even later, I dreaded Sunday evening when the kids went back to their mom's. The silence that filled the house was deafening."

As a divorced man, you are fighting a battle against the desire to get away from reality, fill the gap in your life, and prove you are still attractive. This cycle can be overwhelming and make a terrible situation even worse. You can't make someone love you, so don't obsess over your ex.[2] And don't turn to inappropriate "solutions." Drugs and alcohol are temporary escapes that will destroy you. Younger women are available and often are looking for a man who appears to offer stability. You know the pain of rejection; don't create another victim.

Promiscuous sex can lead to a sexually transmitted disease or result in an unintended pregnancy. And it brings any number of spiritual and emotional consequences. Besides, God outlaws drunkenness and extra-marital sex. So do yourself a favor and keep these urges under control. And while you're at it, recognize that working longer hours won't heal the pain. Even if you become the top sales producer in your territory, at the end of the day you're still a hurting single dad.

I don't say this flippantly, but here's what you need to do: Be a man and face the facts. Tomorrow will come, and with it will come your responsibilities. Your children need your strength, and they need you to provide the practical assistance that life demands. When they are staying with you, they have to get to school. Their laundry needs to be done. Meals need to be prepared. And your children have personal needs at multiple levels that must be met. You have to keep going. You will survive. And you'll do it well—not perfectly, but well.

STARTING A NEW LIFE

Divorce is much more than two people parting ways. I had plans for my family that stretched out for the next forty years. Suddenly I was separated from my wife, her family, her friends, my friends, my lifestyle, and my future. You don't divorce a person; you *lose a life*.

Divorce is difficult under any circumstance. But in some ways it's even more difficult when you confront it honestly. Initially, meeting things head-on increases the pain, but the more open and honest you can be at the outset, the swifter and more certain the healing will be. Here are three keys to getting on with your life:

1. Focus on what needs to be done *today*. Then go ahead and do those things.

2. Hold on to the truth that life goes on and you will begin to heal. Your children are counting on you. You must land on your feet.

3. Rely on God to help you, even to carry you, every step of the way.

In the thirty years that I have practiced karate, I've learned that I can take a whale of a punch. I've been in rounds where I was caught in the face with a kick that sent me to the canvas. Sometimes you see the blow coming, sometimes not. In either case, there is no way to prepare yourself. *Pow!* The blow lands and your head is cloudy. Your vision narrows. You try to shake off the blur and stay in the fight. You stay away from your opponent and lead him to believe you're not hurt. It's a struggle to survive. Getting to the end of the round without being destroyed is all that matters. You focus on the moment because *the fight goes on!* You know the round will end, the pain will go away, and you will survive to fight again.

In a fight, much of this happens instinctively and at lightning speed. In life, there is way too much time to think things over. This is especially true when things are going poorly. We second-guess our words and decisions. We analyze what happened and think up all sorts of alternative scenarios that might have led to a positive outcome. When you find yourself heading down that road, hit the brakes.

Blame is useless. Don't accept it and don't deliver it. Assessing blame is unnecessary and does nothing to help you and your kids heal. A failed marriage is everyone's fault and no one's fault. Mistakes are made. People have problems. Divorce happens.

As single dads, we have to stay on top of things—things like taking care of our children. I've never met a single dad who doesn't love his children more than life itself. We're in a fight, a fight for something far greater than a black belt in martial arts. We're neck-deep in a fight to recover integrity for our families.

I fight daily to protect, nurture, and guide my four children: Jennifer Noel—witty, charming, energetic; Ian Michael—ten thousand comedians out of work and we got Ian, who is also athletic, intelligent, possessing a piercing perception about life; then there's Melissa Paige—musician, dancer, actress, a beautiful, tender woman in the making; and finally, Nicolas Fyodor—his dad in microcosm, heaven help him. These are the beneficiaries of the hard struggle, the fight to stay on top. We want the best for our children. That's why we struggle today and then struggle again tomorrow and the day after that.

LANDING ON YOUR FEET

Here's the truth: There is very little that we actually control. We can't force a spouse to love us, to hang in there with us, or to give the marriage one more chance. It's true that we can control ourselves, but we can't go back and rewrite history. We messed up. We sinned against our ex-wives, who likewise sinned against us. We were *both* wrong, and if we had any humility, we confessed our sins to those we hurt and to God. But that's in the past. What happened happened. So concentrate your thoughts and energies on the one thing that you can still do something about—landing on your feet for the benefit of your kids.

Landing on your feet demands that you address a few basic issues. None of these is easy, but they're all pretty simple.

1. Face the Facts

To move forward in life, we have to face life as it is—not as we wish it were. Before we can gain control and work through the grieving process, we need to squarely face reality. Sometimes reality bites, but the teeth marks will fade in time. So let go of the dream today, once and for all. Grieve its death and accept your situation for what it is.

If you are lonely, you are lonely. If you are hurt, you are hurt. If you made mistakes that caused irreparable brokenness, then you made mistakes. Confess your wrongdoing and seek forgiveness, if you haven't already. And realize that you can't undo what has been done. God knows the pain of your loneliness and he will forgive your mistakes. God understands and will supply the strength when your own strength fails. He is faithful to do these things for us.

In the Bible we read the amazing truth that God's strength is made perfect in our weakness.[3] Being alone, being hurt, being at fault, being the victim of someone else's carelessness—all of these cause sorrow and pain. However, it's not the end of the world. Though you have good reason to feel emotionally battered, you have children, extended family, friends, and a God who are all still with you. Draw strength and wisdom from those who remain on your side.

Find someone you can talk to. Vent. Pray together. Cry out. But carry on. Facing the facts as they are is the first step to dealing with the pain and regaining control. There is a second reason you need to face the facts: If you weren't before, you are now the rock of your family. No one will come to your rescue. Be a man and stand in the gap for your children.

2. Acknowledge Your Shifting Roles

Your marital status has changed, which means that the rest of your life has changed as well. You can't attempt to go on with life as it was before. Your job, children, and friends must take on new roles in your life. This isn't an option, it's reality.

Your Job

Guard your job through your pain and the confusion of emotions you are feeling. You—and your children—need your job.

Most employers will be compassionate to a degree. If your job performance is being affected, take whatever personal time you are allowed to pull yourself together and begin recovery. Yet try to adopt the model of David, the greatest king of ancient Israel. David messed up big-time by committing adultery and then sending his lover's husband to the front lines of battle to be killed. His adultery resulted in the birth of a baby boy, who became deathly ill. David prayed for his son's life to be spared, but the boy died. Once the child was dead, David faced the facts. He cleaned himself up and went on with life while putting away his mourning.[4]

You have to rise up and put away your mourning. You have to resume the role of leading your family. Collect yourself and refuse to wallow in self-pity.

When you do return to work, be careful not to use your colleagues as your sounding board. People care about what you're going through, but they have their own problems. Plus they have work to do. So don't overburden them, even if they keep nodding and smiling when you stop by to talk. Share your pain to the extent that someone asks about it, but remember that they have deadlines to meet and assignments to complete. There is a proper time for mourning, so after work, with a close friend or family member, moan away.[5] Just protect your job.

Employers would rather see you recover than self-destruct. They don't want to lose a good employee. So if you are wise and don't abuse the time you need, they will work with you to allow a few personal days. But remember the bottom line: Don't let your work suffer.

Your Extended Family

The role your extended family plays also will shift after a divorce. Whether they are near or far away, most families want to rally to the cause. But there is no guarantee they will take your side. They may insist that they saw it coming, and they might start placing blame.

You don't need this, since your emotions are already stirred enough. If your family—whether it's your own or your former in-laws—won't keep their mouths shut and lend a hand, keep them at a distance. This involves a tricky bit of relationship juggling. You need the support of your family. You need their help with the children. Your children need the healthy, positive support of aunts, uncles, and grandparents.

However, the children don't need propaganda. They don't need to hear anyone putting either of their parents in a bad light. And they don't ever need to be the objects of manipulation, especially just so someone can make a point. They need to be allowed to just be kids.

Right now you need only a few things from your extended family— the concrete issues of support, time with your children, and other practical assistance. If families—yours or your ex's—don't do this, you must diplomatically reroute their energies or keep them at a distance.

My family was wonderfully supportive. They offered housing, financial assistance, encouragement, help with a job search, and care for the children. But they lived hundreds of miles away, so I couldn't take full advantage of their loving attention. Still, it was much-needed and much-appreciated affirmation and encouragement.

On the other hand, there were times when questions and comments would begin with an accusation: "How could their mother do such a thing? What was she thinking? It's just not right for a mother to act like that." This type of comment only opens the door to gossip and hurt feelings, which will sap your energy. You really don't know why things happened as they did. So redirect the conversation immediately: "I wonder if I could ask a favor. Would you mind helping the kids out by…?" If they don't take the hint, be more direct and tell them to stop playing the blame game.

In short, your relationship with your extended family needs to be utilitarian. You'll have time some other day for the enjoyment of relaxed conversation and the normal give-and-take of relationships. For now it's you who needs assistance.

Your Friends

The role of your friends will shift, much like that of your extended family. Your divorce may well test the true bonds of friendship. You won't have the time to invest in those relationships or the freedom to be as involved as you were before. Your circle of freedom has become more domestically centered. It's fine to occasionally get a sitter and go out or have friends over, but you must consider your children's needs first.

Some friends will now assume you enjoy all the freedom of a single adult without children. They will want you to take a break from your family responsibilities. You do need some R&R but never at the expense of your kids. Don't try to fill your own emotional gaps with "good times." The carefree days before you had children are behind you. Go out with friends, but do it in measured doses and only with things in proper order at home—with the appropriate childcare arrangements and with all necessary responsibilities taken care of.

My friend Rick had a divorced female friend who affirmed his efforts to be the dad his kids needed. He appreciated the encouragement, but he also recognized the danger of falling into a romantic or sexual relationship with another vulnerable single parent. He still needed time to heal from his divorce without the distraction of a new romance. He emphasized, "We definitely needed to keep the friendship a friendship."

Rick was fortunate to have a safe female friend. We need to hear that we are doing a good job with our kids. So surround yourself with the right friends, but be extremely careful. Face the fact that you are vulnerable. Don't let friends feed your anger or your self-pity by choosing sides and stirring contention. You can't afford that distraction right now.

You may also need the practical assistance of several trustworthy friends, as if they were members of your extended family. Be willing to ask for help. You need support. You need sitters you can trust and with whom your children feel comfortable. Friends can be supportive eyes and ears for you. I asked a friend who was a neighbor to keep an eye out for my children after school. If you have a neighbor you trust, enlist his or her help to look in on your kids, especially as they begin the adjustment to being latchkey kids (another reality you have to face).

Friends also can be good listeners and quiet sounding boards. Friends can hold you accountable to help keep you on track. True friends will assist you in your role as a single dad, and you will need to ensure that's the main role they fill.

Your Children

Your kids have new questions and different needs after a divorce. They are hurt, frightened, angry, and confused. They will try to assess blame—often wrongly concluding that *they* are at fault. Though children never need to blame themselves, they often do anyway. It's part of the grieving process. One of my children decided that my wife and I divorced because she quit gymnastics. However nonsensical it may seem to those on the outside, to the child it is very real. Assure your children that they are not at fault, that the divorce was entirely a matter between their mother and you. Divorce is one of those events in life that can rush a child into being an adult. They desperately want to help and to fix things. Do all you can to allow them to remain children.

The first need is to help your children land on their feet. You do that by leading. Get healthy and lead them to health along with you. Part of that process might include counseling—as individuals or as a family. That counseling might come from a pastor or from a professional therapist. Regardless, it's vital that you understand that your children might need counseling.

And they need you to be honest with them—without spilling *all* your guts. If you are crying and hurt, let the children know why. But choose words wisely. My children always put up a force field whenever I go into too-much-information mode. *Oh no! Dad's gonna start talking and he's never gonna stop!* As my children lapse into an information coma, I'm reminded that brief, sympathetic answers are usually the best.

Keep things short and specific. And address their needs when you admit one of your own. Acknowledge what a burden they must feel: "I know you're confused. So am I. But things will work out and in time maybe we'll have a better understanding of all this." Short answers acknowledge and validate their feelings while allowing them to move on.

When you talk about your own feelings and needs, be careful not to cast your ex in a negative light. It's easy to portray her negatively and rationalize that you're doing so only to protect or teach your children. Don't. Instead, focus on yourself. Remove the piece of lumber that is blinding your own eye rather than trying to describe the sliver of error you see stuck in your ex-wife's eye.[6] Even if your former spouse is pursuing an immoral lifestyle, don't go overboard in pointing out her sin. Instead of obsessing on your ex's faults, concentrate on teaching your kids positive values that you want them to adopt. They will see the truth without you preaching a sermon.

I sat with my oldest daughter after her mom had left and told her, "I realize now how hurt your mom had become. And I realize that you had taken too much responsibility for your little brothers. But now I want you to be a little girl for a few more years and let me be the parent." She actually sighed with relief.

But then came the balancing act. Though I wanted her to stay a child, sometimes I needed her maturity in the home. This is a fine line of trial and error. Give your children the same assignments that kids in an intact family would have. It's healthy to have chores. But it's unhealthy for any one person to have too much responsibility for making the household run smoothly. Letting children help with cooking is different from giving them the responsibility of preparing meals. You need to take care of the planning and shopping. Let them assist as they are able with preparation, serving, and cleanup.

"I need you to do the laundry" is different from "You are in charge of keeping all our clothes clean." "Please help your brother get dressed this morning" is different from "You're in charge of getting your brothers and sisters dressed every morning." The idea is to let them be helpers, not surrogate parents, of their younger siblings.

3. Learn to Control Yourself

Recently in reading the dedication of a karate training book, I was reminded of an ancient proverb common to the Chinese and Japanese martial arts: "One who controls others is strong. One who controls himself is mighty." Choose to be mighty for your children by learning how to control yourself. Controlling your reactions and emotions is difficult at best. But it is your responsibility.

When I worked as a prison chaplain, I met two men who failed to control their anger. In both cases they killed their ex-wives and now are in prison. Their children, the innocent parties, are the unintended victims. Because these men failed to control themselves, everyone lost.

Anger is a secondary emotion, an outward manifestation of the pain we're feeling inside. Getting in touch with the pain and facing it head-on is the way to dismiss the anger. So lean into your pain, admit it, process it. Be man enough to be hurt.

4. Get the Outside Help You Need

You need help. I know, I know. You're a man and can leap tall buildings in a single bound. I myself was once such a man—or thought I was. Right after my divorce, however, I was able to stumble into buildings with a single step. I needed help, and fortunately I sought it out.

I was the victim of drastic mood swings. They were affecting my work and my relationship with my kids. I finally went to see a doctor, who prescribed Prozac. The medication stabilized my mood and calmed my panic attacks. Though I had been a martial artist for some thirty years, had attended military school for twelve years, and had served in the military for six years, I had anxiety attacks on every issue from rejection and loneliness to failure to what would become of my sex life if I ever remarried. And what if I *didn't* remarry? I clearly needed help.

One day in the car I caught myself voicing all types of concerns and fears to my teenage daughter Jennifer. Before I knew it, her eyes were filling with tears. "Dad, you need help. And it ain't me." She was right.

When you realize you need outside help, make sure you seek assistance from the right source. Friends can't help with the things for which you need a pastor. And pastors can't help with issues that require medical or psychological attention. Seek help from the proper source. And seek help for your *whole* person—mentally, emotionally, physically, and spiritually. You're probably not the best judge of how you're doing in those areas, especially when you're still reeling from a divorce.

I was depressed long before I knew it. When my marriage fell apart, I tried to fix it. When that failed, I sought to pull myself together. Eventually, I realized there was no simple solution. The emotional drain of the divorce, the stress of my new single status, the carryover of brokenness from before the divorce all came into view. As I worked on one issue, three more came to light. I needed a complete overhaul. This required the services of a team of conspirators.

My spiritual health is primary to the health of my family and to my own life. So I put myself in the care of two pastors. I began counseling with them in order to have accountability, spiritual support, advice, and repair. Both men had similar perspectives but expressed their views differently. By blending their ideas and following their advice, I was able to recover a healthy spiritual perspective and avoid relying on my own judgment, which was badly scarred from the battle at hand.

Get with your pastor and be vulnerable. Listen, pray, and follow his advice. The hard part is often disciplining ourselves to do what pastors advise. If you seek their help and they provide grounded, reasonable advice, then follow it.

Keep your head in the Scriptures. You need the solid wisdom and guidance of God's teachings. You may feel you just can't read because your mind is too full. You might feel you already know what is being said. No matter what, read it. Little steps are fine. Not studying will further weaken an already weak structure.

Don't neglect prayer. When you are hurting, pray. When you get angry, pray. When you're feeling lonely, pray. Confess your feelings to God, pray for others in your same position, pray for your family, pray for your former spouse. Pray.

Guard against negative influences from outside sources like music or television. Keep your focus on comforting, quieting music and entertainment programming.

Friends can help as sounding boards, but they are not professionals and they often confuse advice and opinion. You can seek out certain friends for wise counsel. However, know that friends have limitations.

And remember that friends and coworkers don't mind hearing about your issues in the right balance and the proper setting. But don't bleed all over these fine folks. Counselors, pastors, psychologists, doctors, and psychiatrists are the professionals you need to bleed on. They can deal with the mess and clean things up. Don't bleed on those who aren't trained to deal with it.

As well as needing spiritual and emotional assistance, I needed to improve my physical health—especially diet and rest. Controlling my diet was a life's work in progress, so I just continued working at eating right. And rest? Now there's another story. As a single dad I was on the run constantly. Demands for my attention were overwhelming. So how could I get more rest?

I discovered that rest is more than sleep. Rest is relaxation, recreation, or even a pause to clear your mind. Rest is taking a few minutes in my car to close my eyes, breathe a few deep, cleansing breaths, and think about something positive—such as the warm smiles of my kids. Rest can be a five-minute prayer of praise to God. Rest is slowing down within while the pace continues without. Rest becomes a learned habit.

Again, seek out the help you need. If you're not getting on top of things, see your doctor. If he recommends a psychiatrist, psychologist, or counselor, follow the doctor's advice. Don't be embarrassed. Be healthy.

5. Hold Your Head Up and Move On

When my wife left, I was in too much pain to look forward. I was a basket case. I could hardly tie my shoes. But I realized I had too many responsibilities that would suffer if I got bogged down in looking back. I couldn't undo what had been done, so it was time to move on. That's easy to write, but doing it was one of the most difficult tasks I've ever faced.

The martial arts taught me a great deal about life. In a battle, every moment is meaningful. A fighter has to focus on the immediate objective and refocus and refocus and refocus. With each frame, we adjust and keep moving forward. We don't change objectives. We don't look back. We move forward.

Even in the most painful moment, there is something to be thankful for. When training for my black belt, I would become so fatigued and so pained that I wanted to quit. I was forty years old. I could quit and folks would understand. But that would be the easy way out. Legendary football coach Vince Lombardi once said, "Fatigue makes cowards of us all."[7] Pain and fatigue help us justify quitting.

Being a single dad means you'll get less sleep. It means you'll have more work to do around the house. It means less income and more expenses, and it might mean working longer hours or taking on a second job. All of this adds up to fatigue, and that's just the physical part. Emotional fatigue is a given.

Given the pain and the weariness, single dads have to focus away from the pain and on something that will keep them moving forward and making steady progress. It will be slow in coming, but each small success will feed the next, and eventually the successes will grow while the pain diminishes.

The Bible is full of paradoxes, things that are counterintuitive but true nonetheless. A biblical paradox that applies in this circumstance regards being disciplined by the negative turns in life: "No discipline seems pleasant at the time, but painful. Later on, however, it produces a harvest of righteousness and peace for those who have been trained by it."[8]

You're going through a time of discipline. It's unpleasant, no question about it. But let the discipline do its work in making you a stronger, more effective father for your kids. If you can't maintain the necessary focus for your own benefit, then do it for your children.

Survival Tips

Take the Pledge

You have begun to recognize areas in which your kids need you to get control, take charge, and lead them in healing and moving forward in life. It helps, at the beginning of this process, to write down a few things you are committing yourself to. Take a few moments to begin such a list right now. This will serve as a visual reminder of both the new realities of life and your duties and commitments to your children.

The following statement of commitment summarizes an immediate goal and a focal point for your actions and your thinking. It allows you to answer one question: "What am I willing to do *today* to be the best dad I can possibly be?" Anything we intend to do well must first have total commitment. Committing to being the best single dad you can be is your most important responsibility to your family and to yourself. Are you willing to commit to the trial-and-error process it takes to let go of self and commit fully to your children? If so, fill in your name below and sign this statement of commitment:

I, _____, in recognition of the importance and difficulty of being a top-quality single dad, solemnly commit to making this duty foremost in my personal journey. I will revisit my commitment on a daily basis as I ask God for the strength to move forward in my own life and in leading my children.

Signed: _____

Date: _____

SINGLE PARENTING IS INSANE

A Fresh Look at the Solo-Dad Job Description

As I WAS BEGINNING my new role as a single dad, I would have killed for a detailed job description. Parenting as a two-member team is tough enough, but single parenting is absolutely insane. It's probably better that there is no written job description for single dads. If we had one, we might run away and hide rather than stay put and shoulder the responsibility.

When I say that single parenting is insane, I don't mean that it gets crazy every now and then. I mean it's *really insane*. It was never intended. It takes two people to conceive a baby and at least a small tribe to raise one. A family centers on a male and a female. Take one of those elements away and what remains is seriously limited. The idea of a single dad was never built into the program.

A single dad needs to be much more than just a father to his kids. You must also be a male mom. Whether your kids are with you full time or just part of the time, you need to develop skills, habits, and abilities that don't come easily but that your kids desperately need.

God has built leadership, provision, instruction, and discipline into the basic male model. Dads charge down the path of life focused on the big things and not overly concerned about the small details along the way. Dads push their children toward improvement; they coach and correct their children. Kids need all of this. But great dads go a step further and learn to balance their natural inclinations with other skills and qualities that help build balanced, healthy relationships with their children.

My former wife and I tended to balance each other out, especially when it came to discipline. It was a good cop–bad cop balance. I was the bad cop. I scolded and raised Cain. She came behind and explained the intent of my ravings. She helped the kids see that I was demanding because I loved them and wanted the best for them. She encouraged our children to make amends with their barking dog of a dad and renew relationship through forgiveness. Then I lavished them with love and mercy, the way God receives us. It was a true team effort.

But sadly, once my ex was gone, my kids had only the bad cop to deal with. What now? How could I become the good cop *and* the bad cop at the same time?

The Insane Job Description

A single dad has to lead, provide, instruct, and discipline. But he must also nurture and encourage with the gentle grace that seems to be the gift God has given women. Since a single father needs to cover both roles when caring for his children, let's look at a man's natural strengths as well as his need to cultivate the parenting skills that don't come as naturally.

I am the sole parent responsible for the daily management and well-being of my children. I'm the only role model in the home. I am the teacher who must instruct my children in the virtues and values that I deem important. I'm the captain of the laundry, the family chef, and the chauffeur. I am the lone authority figure. I am the family's chief warrior. I am also the peacemaker, the priest, the physician, and the counselor.

A single dad must cover *all* the bases. This undertaking demands commitment, maturity, energy, and patience. It's a path of constant self-assessment and forgiveness for your own shortcomings. It requires honesty with yourself and with your children. It's a job no one wants because it's a job that no one person can handle. But now you've got to handle it.

As the lone adult when your children are in your care, you're facing issues you didn't have to think about when you were married. Now they're major matters requiring your full attention and energy.

After my divorce, I got an education the first time one of my kids got sick. I was at work when I got a call from the school nurse. It was up to me to get my son home and in bed. That was just the beginning. When I got him settled and pumped full of medication, I realized I wasn't being very nice.

I was operating in default mode—being a take-charge guy, covering all the logistical needs. But I was blind to my son's crying need at that moment: He needed tender nurture. Taking time to soothe and cuddle doesn't always come naturally to men. But when tiny tummies are upset, there is great need for tenderness as well as medication. If I overlooked tenderness, what else was I missing by a simple lack of awareness? If a doctor had displayed my bedside manner, he wouldn't have remained my doctor for long.

The need to improve on the basic dad default mode extends beyond times of illness to such ordinary activities as doing homework. When my kids need help with schoolwork, I tend to look their papers over, tell them the process for getting the right answers, then expect them to jump right on it. On the other hand, their mom was great at pulling up a chair and truly helping with homework, not merely pointing out what needed to be corrected then barking out a command to be quick about it. She was there for them emotionally as well as in the practical matter of providing help.

We'll explore this balancing act—playing the roles of both dad *and* mom—further in the next chapter.

Time to Grow Up

I have always loved Peter Pan, since growing up was never my chief goal in life. In our society we continue to play at life and seek amusements long beyond childhood. In a team of two parents, there is some room for childishness since one spouse can cover for the other. But in a team of one, that luxury disappears. A single dad can no longer hang on to his childish ways. It's time to grow up.

Single parenthood demands selflessness and consistency. In short, you must be willing to pour yourself out as a sacrificial servant to those you love. Here's how Jesus put it: "Greater love has no one than this, that he lay down his life for his friends."[1]

That sounds daunting, but there's good news as well. Setting aside your own interests and convenience for the welfare of your children is an act of sacrifice that God honors and blesses. He will see you through as you attempt to give yourself wholly to the task. No longer can a single dad afford to focus on his own agenda. His agenda now has to center on his children. The task is both exhausting and rewarding. You'll become a stronger person who will know how to meet the needs of those you love the most.

A significant shift comes with simple family rituals. When I was married, I prayed with my kids at bedtime, then my wife would tuck them in. Now as a single dad, I realized I needed to do both jobs at bedtime. I had to not only pray with my kids but read to them, hug them, snuggle with them, and nurture them.

This shift also affects how we use our personal time. At first, after my divorce, I didn't want to give up the freedom to go out when I wanted. I enjoyed shooting pool and hanging out with friends. As I got deeper into my new life as a single dad, though, I realized that every time I left the house to get a break, my kids—ages six to fifteen when I divorced—were left alone. I had to start evaluating what my being gone meant to my children, and much of it was not good.

For one, it meant that one of the kids had to temporarily fill in as the adult—a difficult position for a child who was already feeling insecure after the divorce. Children of divorce often feel a responsibility to do something to fix the brokenness. So rather than feeling like they're just baby-sitting younger siblings, for instance, they might feel they are actually filling in for a missing parent. It's a heavy emotional responsibility for a kid to handle.

Once children lose one parent to divorce, they carry a greater fear of losing the other parent. It now looms as a real possibility, not just a fleeting thought. If Dad goes out with the guys, the children are afraid he might not come back. This doesn't mean we single dads can never go out, but it might mean giving up some hobbies, amusements, and bad habits in order to be there for our kids. Our children need to be reassured that we are dependable, that we're on their side, and that we're not going to disappear.

My friend Ron made a special effort to keep his life family-centered even when his children were not with him. "I had to evaluate my whole lifestyle," he says. "My children might be with their mom, but they still might need to talk to their dad. So I made a point to be home during the week just like I was before the divorce. If they needed to talk to me, they could pick up the phone and call."

I wouldn't necessarily advise staying home every night just in case your kids *might* call, but it would be a good idea to at least carry a cell phone so your kids can reach you any time they need you.

Ron also took a hard look at his dating habits. "I dated some, but very carefully," he says. "I made certain that the kids didn't meet anyone I was dating. They didn't need to be afraid of losing their dad to some other woman. They also didn't need to meet someone and become fond of her only to lose her when we quit dating."

Ron admits those choices were difficult. "I'm a people person," he says. "But it was worth the sacrifice for my family."

Another friend, a single mom, offers this helpful perspective: Divorce is not the end of a family but a different phase in the life of that family. We single dads need to remember that family goes on, and our kids need a dad 24/7. Keeping our children as protected and stable as possible in an undesirable situation should direct our focus.

OUR NEED TO BE AFFIRMED

Affirmation should be a part of every social setting. Families, classrooms, churches, friends getting together—anyplace where there is relationship there should also be a natural flow of affirmation. The need to be affirmed is universal, and in and of itself this need is not destructive. Yet many of us fail to realize that our desire to be affirmed can put a lot of pressure on others. An overbearing need for affirmation is often at the root of marital pressures that can drive a spouse away. A man seeking affirmation can channel that need into unhealthy expressions, including a demanding sexual appetite, egoism that creates competition between spouses, or a habit of asking questions designed to seek a spouse's constant approval.

After a divorce, when we're feeling rejected and unloved, the drive to find affirmation can overwhelm us. If our wives rejected us, we think that must mean we're no longer desirable. In an effort to quiet the panic, we can overdo it in seeking positive input from others—especially women. That, in turn, can lead to messy and unintended emotional entanglements and even inappropriate sexual involvement. We need to find a balance by seeking a healthy, mutual give-and-take to replace the self-focused, one-sided pursuit of affirmation that sucks others dry.

Recognize that you are all right. Sure, your wife may have thought differently, but you have friends and colleagues who remain loyal to you. They see positive qualities in you. And most important, you are all right because God created you in his image.[2] Rather than seeking your identity in the opinions of those around you, seek your identity in God's love for you. Call to mind God's grace and mercy to all who confess their sin and wrongdoing to him, claiming the forgiveness made possible through God's Son. See yourself as a forgiven, complete, valued child of God. Your children need you to be emotionally and spiritually strong, a dad who has things together—as much as that's possible right now.

Great advice, right? But how do we take steps to appropriately fill the void left by divorce? We start by first acknowledging that the need for affirmation is real and God given. Don't try to be a tough guy and say, "Hey, I don't need anybody else," because that's a lie. God made us to be relational beings. We need each other, and that's never a sign of weakness.

Once you've acknowledged your need for affirmation, start to determine *appropriate* sources of affirmation. The first source is God himself. Seek his comfort in prayer and by reading Scripture. You are made in his image, and he didn't make any mistakes. Replay this truth in your mind and accept yourself as you are. Memorize a few verses of Scripture (such as Genesis 1:27 and Psalm 139:14) that affirm these truths. Write these verses on three-by-five-inch cards and post them where you'll see them often—your bathroom mirror, your dashboard, at the office.

Other sources of affirmation are people in your inner circle, starting with family and close friends, as discussed in the previous chapter. They can become your biggest cheerleaders. There's nothing like a friend patting you on the back to say you're doing a good job, or saying that he's praying for you, to encourage you on this road.

Another people source is the church—a group of people who love Jesus and who seek to follow his model. These are compassionate people who understand your need for honest affirmation. Also, a local church may have a ministry to singles or divorced people, offering special classes, seminars, events, and support groups.

There are other sources of affirmation. Your job might be one of them. Think of your paycheck as not only a way to support your family, but as affirmation for a job well done. But don't put too many eggs in this basket. Many men seek proof of their value in their paycheck.

When I was in sales, I saw too many men looking for affirmation in closing the deal that brought the biggest commission. Outdoorsmen might look for affirmation in the biggest fish or largest trophy buck to hang on their den wall. The real reward comes when we wean ourselves from the need to be constantly affirmed by our achievements or by those around us.

As you find balance in this area, regularly assess your successes, no matter how small. Treat yourself occasionally to a nice lunch or a new CD. You might also find affirmation in certain activities, such as a favorite hobby, sports, or entertainment. Think of these as occasional rewards for tackling the demanding job of being a single dad.

Affirmation is good, but don't get consumed by it. If you're spending every night on the phone with a friend, seeking affirmation while your kids fend for themselves, you're taking it too far. If you're showing up regularly at several church singles gatherings in the hope of scouting out a new hottie or spending every Saturday with a support group, your kids are probably wondering when they'll see you again. Pick and choose your sources of affirmation wisely. Be discerning. Ask a close friend or a pastor to hold you accountable in this area. Meet with him regularly and tell him where you're seeking affirmation and get his feedback. Tell him to let you know when you might be going overboard.

Here's a good rule of thumb: Ask yourself if pursuing a particular source of affirmation will help or hinder your best effort to care for your children. If it's a hindrance, tell it good-bye—unless it's your source of income, of course.

Learning to balance your need for affirmation with your responsibilities as a single dad is difficult. As we've noted, it isn't just natural, but it's necessary.

About now you probably feel like screaming or crying or turning in your resignation. This insane job description is about to drive you stark raving mad. But before you run amuck, stop and take a deep breath. Hold on to this truth: The Creator of the universe wants you to succeed as a father. Your heavenly Father is with you every step of the way. And if God is with you, then who could possibly stand in your way?[3] Ask God to give you the faith and confidence you need to move forward in self-sacrifice, in nurture, and in wisdom to become the dad your kids need.

My friend Frank probably said it best: "You're now a dad *and* a mom, so the best thing is to spend time with your children. Bond with them! It keeps you compatible. It allows for better communication. Being a good parent must become your consuming passion in life."

And as you continue to make strides as a single dad, you'll be affirmed in your successes.

Survival Tips

What Are Your Priorities?

The following questions will help you think through the priorities in your solo-dad job description. If you desire to grow and become proficient in this demanding new role, this type of self-assessment will go a long way toward achieving that goal. It will also save you from some pitfalls along the way. Feel free to adapt these questions to fit your needs and your particular circumstances.

1. Aside from having lost the company of your spouse, what is your greatest fear in being alone?

2. What are your immediate needs? After you list those needs, make a second list of the needs for which you can ask others for help. Who can you ask, and what makes each of these people a good choice?

3. Are there personal sacrifices that you don't want to make because you don't like giving up the things you really enjoy? What can you do to address those issues? If you have pinpointed areas that indicate a selfish agenda, how can you move to a place of putting your kids' needs ahead of your own?

4. Is your need for affirmation in the aftermath of rejection leading you into dangerous waters? How can you avoid compromised words and situations both now and in the future?

5. What is a reasonable amount of time for you to devote to personal recreation and relaxation each week? Are you willing to discuss that with your children and to take their input to heart?

ROUNDING OFF SOME ROUGH EDGES

Striking a Balance Between Drill Sergeant and Grandma

NINE OUT OF TEN dads agree: It's great to be a guy. And the lone hold-out agreed the next day, after he'd had some time to think it over.

It really is great to be a guy, and God didn't make you a guy by accident. So get out there and be a guy for all the world to see. But at the same time, realize that males—like everyone else—have natural strengths and weaknesses. And we need to be aware of how our inherent weaknesses and blind spots might affect our children.

A single dad is, by definition, single. He's the only parent the kids have when they are in his care. What's missing during those times is the gentleness and grace that moms bring to family life. A woman's homey touch balances the testosterone of the male existence. A dad will stand at the stove with no shirt, wearing baggy boxer shorts, checking on a pot of stew with a beer in one hand and a dripping spatula in the other.

There is a time and a place for earthy maleness. We'll talk about that later, so don't throw this book across the room just yet. But remember that when we're on Dad Duty, we must think seriously about the big picture—especially when Mom is no longer part of that picture. There is a time for gentleness, manners, and tenderness. Without a mom around to balance Dad's uncivilized maleness, the whole house can lean to one side. Before it flips over, try some timely self-assessment.

Let's say one of your kids comes home from school with a fever or from soccer practice with a sprained ankle. The typical guy response is "Suck it up." I have caught myself almost bragging about how many times my nose has been broken as a result of practicing martial arts. But after some self-assessment, I realized that a daughter with an upset stomach probably doesn't need to hear stories about how someone else not only had nausea but diarrhea too—*all at the same time!* Maybe she needs a soft crook of an arm to rest her head in and a little comfort to know that she will be all right.

There is a time for toughness but never at the expense of tender hearts. I had to do some pretty serious backtracking and offer some gentle apologies for my callous attitude the first few times my little ones were ill. I still find myself wanting them to "take it like a soldier." However, I resist the tough-guy advice and find the grace to be tender and nurturing.

It makes sense that being a successful dad requires that we look at the typical male's strengths and weaknesses. Now that you're parenting solo, you'll need to balance and complement your natural manly abilities with other not-so-natural skills. And that will take some practice. Getting a clear idea of the things that don't come naturally will help you compensate and actively pursue solutions, often involving the assistance of others.

All men are different, and yet we're all the same. Our common qualities vary in manner of expression, but they are part of the basic nature of being male. Let's take a look at some of the most pronounced aspects of being male.

LEADING WITHOUT CONTROLLING

A primary male tendency is that we want to lead. While a man may tend to follow another's lead in other group settings, he wants to lead his family. And when he fails to lead, it usually results in disaster, limiting the family's ability to fire on all cylinders. This is not to demean the leadership abilities of women; it's just to acknowledge that men have an innate drive to lead.

Children, likewise, have an innate need to belong to a family or some other family-like group. Street gangs are evidence of the natural human tendency to gather into some form of a tribal group. Kids who are searching for a cultural identity congregate around the strongest male leader. One strength of being a single dad is that your family will naturally rally around you if you will simply stand strong. In short, you have been invited to set the pace for your kids. Take advantage of this by setting the example for the way you want your children to live.

As we consider the need to lead, remember that there's a big (and crucial) difference between leading and controlling. Many men have difficulty leading because they feel they need to wield absolute control to do so. It's time to eliminate that idea. A leader leads most effectively by setting an example. A leader listens, observes, and makes wise decisions in the best interest of his family, often after seeking wise counsel first and then searching the minds and needs of those he serves—his children. Leadership is serving the group, not controlling the group. Control becomes an issue when a dad is serving himself instead of his children. A dad's job is not to pursue his own agenda but his family's. A godly leader looks out for the best interests of the group. In a family, this means giving everyone the freedom to choose how to respond to your leadership.[1]

God has given us a clear model to follow. He advises us, provides for us, and protects us, but he doesn't control us. We are free to choose our response. So it should be with a dad's leadership in the family. Advise, provide, protect, but don't insist on total compliance. Give your children room to be individuals. Punish them when needed. Admonish them when needed. God does the same to us.[2] But don't insist on subservience. When you do, you're controlling, not leading.

My oldest daughter came to me when she was fourteen and asked if she could dye her hair blue. I love my daughter, but I didn't want her to have blue hair. I felt that going around with blue hair might send the wrong signal to the world about the kind of person she is. But I gave her the freedom to make her own decision. I said, "Sure, honey. If you want to dye your hair and it doesn't violate any school dress code, then go ahead. I really like your hair the way it is, but if this is important to you, then you have my permission."

She dyed her hair blue. I was okay with her new look, but some folks outside our family took a different view. My daughter came home from church a few days later looking hurt and confused.

"Dad, am I rebellious?" she asked. Her tone broke my heart.

"Why do you ask that?"

"The kids at church said I was rebellious for dying my hair blue."

"Well, Jennifer, you asked me first and I gave you permission. A rebel goes against authority. If I had said no and you had done it anyway, that would have been rebellion. So no, you're *not* rebellious. Tell them you're just trying out a different hair color. You're not the type who blindly follows the crowd, and that's a good thing."

Jennifer enjoyed her blue hair for a while. Then, as her hair grew out and the dye faded, so did the excitement. She enjoyed the experiment and then moved on.[3]

If I had insisted on exercising total control, my daughter would have grudgingly avoided blue hair during that school year, but a few years later as a young adult she might still wonder what it feels like to really cut loose and experiment. And she might be drawn to something far more harmful than blue hair. Today Jennifer is a college student working her way toward law school. She enjoyed the freedom to get the playfulness and experimentation out of her system as a teenager; now she's on to more important things. Neither blue hair nor her natural hair color means a thing. What's important is that my daughter knows in her heart what is good and what is not. Raise your children with the right values and lead them in right actions. Be the model they need; don't settle for mere lip service to godly leadership. If you are faithful in serving them as leader of the family, your children will find their way past neon hair dye and multiple piercings and baggy pants to more important things.

Leadership is both a natural quality and a practiced skill. The desire and basic orientation already are in place. The skill needs to be learned, however, and then perfected. Part of that process includes taking responsibility for our actions and decisions rather than trying to pass the buck.

Adam, in the book of Genesis, had no problem with the *idea* of leadership. However, he fell far short when it came time to exercise that responsibility. "This wife you gave me, she's defective," he told God, in essence.[4] In other words, Adam argued that it was all God's fault. Or maybe it was Eve's fault. But it was never Adam's fault.

Don't fall for the lie. Stand up and be counted. Take responsibility for your life and for the welfare of your family. You're the only parent around when your kids are in your care, so you *must* lead! Your children will look to you for direction, role modeling, appropriate boundaries, and affirmation. What's more, they will seriously test your resolve. They lost the home life they were familiar with. They lost the comforting and reassuring presence of two full-time parents. So they are hurt and angry and probably scared. They are quick to blame someone, often themselves, for the divorce. And they will act out their anger. They'll also test boundaries and experiment with borderline behavior just to see if you have the right mettle. In doing this, they want to find out if you'll be strong—or if you'll run.

Children whose lives have been torn apart by divorce need someone to hold things together. They need to feel that life has not come completely unglued. A single dad can meet that need through his stable leadership.

No one submits willingly to any authority if they don't think that authority has their best interests at heart. Conversely, if people think a leader has their best interests at heart, they will follow him even through adversity. If you earn your children's respect, they will naturally honor your leadership.

Remember, leaders lead from the front. They set the pace, provide an example, and operate within the rules. Show your kids the kind of life you want them to adopt. Model the behavior you desire in their lives. You want a clean house? Pick up a mop. Demonstrate the behavior you want and sell the benefits. Then when you issue a housecleaning command, the kids will line up for service.

My friend Frank echoes the need for dads to be leaders: "After a divorce, it's possible to get too close in some ways to our children. We use them as a sounding board or as a buddy. It's much more important to be a leader. Spend some of your time being a buddy. But *always* be a leader."

Discipline and Tenderness

In addition to being leaders, men possess a natural tendency to discipline their kids. Men tend to be more comfortable setting boundaries and enforcing rules, providing a serious reprimand or punishment when needed. This is good, because children need clear boundaries. After a divorce, kids—especially the high-energy and strong-willed ones—will test the strength and resolve of the custodial parent. The family has been broken, so the children want to see if the remaining structure is going to hold up. Dads serve their children by patiently and purposefully standing their ground as they provide reasonable boundaries.

My oldest daughter, Jennifer, was fifteen when her mom left. At the time, she was a disciplined athlete and a dedicated gymnast. Almost instantly, though, she fell apart and began acting out her hurt. She took up smoking cigarettes and skipping school. While I was a dad who allowed my kids room to be themselves, I also drew definite lines on certain issues. I didn't come down hard on the smoking; I simply discussed my feelings and reminded Jennifer of the health issues involved. I gave her room to decide for herself. This was a judgment call on my part.

However, skipping school was a much bigger issue. This was not just missing a few days due to emotional distress. Jennifer was lying about her whereabouts when she was supposed to be at school. Trust is a basic requirement for a family to function well and is nonnegotiable in our family. I explain to my kids that trust and freedom go hand in hand. If they want more freedom, they have to earn my trust. Since Jennifer had broken that trust, I couldn't give her the freedom she desired. Being a solo dad, I couldn't operate without a high level of trust. I had four latchkey kids, and I didn't want to run a jail. So we all needed trust.

On the issue of lying about skipping classes, Jennifer was testing boundaries. *Wham!* The hammer fell. She was grounded for deceiving me. After the tears and anger, though, she thanked me for providing her with some boundaries.

Genuine love and wise discipline are inseparable. To truly love a child you must diligently discipline that child, but you must always do so in love. And as you stand strong, remember that discipline is training; it's not striking or ridiculing. While I am a proponent of appropriate corporal discipline, I am not a proponent of abuse. There is a stage in a child's development when his or her ability to reason is not yet well developed, and respect for authority comes from an understanding of potential harm. The pain and disappointment of a spanking clearly communicate this to young children. But eventually children outgrow this form of discipline. The timing of that change seems to come around the age of nine or ten.

These things might very well look different in your family. So review your own policies on discipline and take an active approach to establishing your authority, *always* disciplining in love.[5] When discipline is exercised in the context of love, you're demonstrating tenderness and nurture. A Quaker father, after spanking his child, would take the child with him and they would spend the day together. Dads find it easy to be rough-and-tumble. Tenderness and nurture don't come as readily. I'm not a huggy person. I'm much more comfortable with a karate kick. But I've had to learn to hug and hold my children tenderly after discipline. A dad is often striking a balance between drill sergeant and grandmother.

MAKING BETTER DECISIONS

Most men are making difficult decisions every day at work. When they get home, though, many married men defer decisions to their wives. Perhaps men become weary of decision making and just want a break in the evening. But after a divorce there is no one to defer to. You're now both dad and home front decision-maker, and every well-run organization relies on a great decision-maker at the top. Your family is no exception.

Don't hesitate to be bold in making decisions. A wrong choice can always be amended or corrected later when more information comes to light. So keep moving forward, correcting your mistakes as you go along. Be a confident decision-maker and then be humble enough to admit when you're wrong.

Since you no longer have your wife as a sounding board, prayer partner, and fellow decision-maker, you'll need to seek wise counsel from other trusted friends or family members. These confidants can share their advice and help you avoid a potentially hazardous decision. If you charge forward without consultation, decision making can be impulsive. You're more likely to make shortsighted decisions based on feelings rather than wisdom. By talking through key decisions with a friend or support group, you will gain needed perspective. It's easy to overlook certain details when everything comes from your own limited point of view.

Here are a couple of areas to consider as you work to improve your decision making.

Long-Range Versus Short-Range

Men tend to focus far ahead on long-range goals and objectives, leaving the immediate details to someone else. Women seem to be much more aware of the here and now of daily living. For example, some dads will set up college funds for their young children but fail to notice that they have outgrown their shoes. Moms tend to see things like outgrown shoes and lunches that need to be made and other typical daily needs of their families, but some may give little thought to possible needs in the distant future.

Single dads need to learn to maintain two perspectives simultaneously, keeping one eye on the current situation and the other looking into the future. Dads need to look down at the trail immediately in front of them as they barrel into the future. This dual process is demanding and tiring but also essential for safe travel.

Kids have many important daily needs. A dad may be prone to saying, "Don't they see I love them? I go to work every day to provide for them!" Moms will bend down and give the children a hug. A solo dad needs to do both.

Functional Versus Aesthetic

Single dads must become aware of *all* of their children's needs—physical, mental, emotional, and spiritual. As the sole on-site provider of love and affection, Dad has to dig deep to become more aware of the little things that make life special.

I remember giving money to my children so they could buy lunch at school. I felt I was providing for their lunch needs. But they needed more than nourishing meals; they needed to feel cared for.

One day my youngest, then six years old, came home and said, "Jimmy's mom makes him the coolest lunches." I heard some envy in Nico's voice. Then it occurred to me that a made lunch was much more personal, communicating a parent's loving touch. I challenged myself to start making cool lunches for my kids. I realized this was another way of saying, "I love you. You are special to me." To date I've made 5,760 lunches. Some were cooler than others.

Some men view divorce as welcome emancipation from the feminizing influence of their former wives. Now they can be slobs and make loud bodily noises and walk around in ratty T-shirts. There is no woman around to make an issue out of such behavior.

But what about your kids? Whether you have sons or daughters or both, children appreciate the gentle civilizing touches of a mother. When they are with you, they still want to feel that things haven't degenerated into the chaos of an indoor landfill.

Here are a few quick questions to help you assess whether you need to rein things in a bit. Do you serve all your family meals in front of the television? Is everyone showing up for dinner without having put on a full set of clothing? When one of your kids is searching for a clean shirt, is it more likely to be found hanging in a closet or buried underneath the pile of laundry that hasn't been touched in weeks?

Singer-songwriter John Prine discussed his divorce while introducing a song on a live album. He said that after his wife left, he and a friend nailed a toy train set to the dining room table "because I could."[6]

No woman around, and immediately the little boy inside the dad comes out full strength. The truth is that a male is generally more functional than aesthetic in his approach to life. If it seems to work, why go out of your way to try something else? And why waste your time prettying things up?

Well, for one, because life is much more than function. God made trees for two reasons. The Bible says he made some to bear fruit, an entirely functional purpose, and others that are simply "pleasing to the eye."[7] From God's standpoint, aesthetics are important!

I'm the last guy to give advice in this area. In college, I brought my bicycle indoors and stood it up on its end in a corner of my room. I called it a Christmas bike because I had no money for a tree. The girl I was dating took one look at the bike with a sheet around the base and suggested I hang some tinsel on it. I didn't see the need. To me the bike served the purpose. It filled the tree void. To her it needed decoration. Two opposite ways of viewing the same thing.

Single dads must be careful to rise above mere functionality. Some men actually rebel against the trappings of femininity that were imposed on their worlds during their years of marriage. But your children need the balance of both worlds—function and beauty. If you have little girls, you'll find out that having clean clothes available is not the only issue. You are expected to sort the colors and read the washing instructions label inside the collar. (Yes, they really do have clear instructions on a tag in the clothing.) Kids appreciate the care that comes with adding that extra, caring touch. Throwing the whole pile into the washer and setting the temperature to "hot" won't cut it.

In short, dads need to fight male myopia and add the balance that was lost after the divorce. The things your former wife did that you never really noticed or thought about were actually her way of balancing the scale. Don't be afraid to borrow from her wisdom, even though she is no longer your wife. Or check with your mom or sister or talk to a friend. Ask a woman what she would add to your home in the way of aesthetics and other civilizing touches. Achieving this type of balance will only make you a better, stronger servant and leader in your home.

Survival Tips

Blessed Are the Flexible

Help your children adapt to the changes that come with divorce by taking a look at some ways you can be both Dad and Mom. Remember, standing strong does not mean being stubborn. Blessed are the flexible for they shall not be broken.

To follow is a list of traits that tend to be in opposition (or balance, depending on your perspective). Use these for continued self-assessment and to help you identify your own strengths and weaknesses as your family's leader. Take each pairing and determine what course of action you can take in order to move toward balance.

- Leader / Team Member
- Disciplinarian / Nurturer
- Decision-Maker / Mediator
- Looking Far Ahead / Seeing the Next Step
- Functional / Aesthetic
- Standing Strong / Being Flexible

YOU AND YOUR DAUGHTER

Girls Are Great,
and They're Also Really Different

I HAVE TWO daughters, and I wouldn't trade them for the world. But raising them alone was no day at the beach. The difficulty of this task didn't hit me full force until their mom had been out of the house for close to six months. That's when I got *the phone call.*

I was home after work when Paige, my younger daughter, called me from school. She was clearly distressed over something.

"What's the matter, honey?" I asked.

"Where's Mom?" she was able to ask in a weak voice, struggling to keep her composure.

"Paige," I replied, "I don't know for sure. She's somewhere in San Antonio, but I don't know where she works."

"Well, where's Jennifer?"

"Jennifer's at track practice. Baby, what's wrong?"

"I started," Paige whispered. Then she began to cry.

She "started" what? Volleyball? Ahhh. *Started!* The light came on. I was totally unprepared. I had been trying to cultivate my feminine side, but this was totally outside my area of expertise. Still, as the on-duty parent, I had to do something.

I'm a dad, I thought, *the resourceful type, brave enough to walk into the teeth of danger, into the shadowy unknown. I'll figure this out if it kills me.*

I went out and bought my daughter a rose, a card, and a little certificate declaring her a special child of God and containing a statement she could use to offer herself as a budding woman in service to God. I put all of these mementos on her pillow, and we had a cozy chat and hug when she came home from school. Whew, that was a close call.

At least, that's what I thought. A few years later I overheard my daughters talking about this episode. As they giggled, I asked what was so funny.

"Dad," Jennifer began, "do you remember when Paige called about her first period?"

"Yes," I said, "and I thought I did a pretty good job."

"Oh, you did great," Jennifer said with a mischievous laugh. "You bought the rose and the card and stuff. You only forgot one thing—pads!" She fell over on the bed she was laughing so hard. In fact, both girls had a nice laugh at my expense. But there you have it. I believe Lucille Ball said it best in the movie *Yours, Mine and Ours:* A man can shop and prepare meals and take care of his family, but he can never be a mom.

I did give it the old college try though. On my first Mother's Day as a single dad, I received a wonderful vote of confidence as my children teamed together to get me a Mother's Day gift. Yet the truth is that a man can never fully replace a mom. My friend Rick remembers his daughter's first period. "Sometimes my daughter and I talk about that day," he says. "Usually we laugh. Sometimes we hold each other and cry. It's tough knowing that no matter how hard you try, a dad can sometimes never be enough."

Here's a thought: Though you may have many issues with your ex-spouse, try with all your might to support the mom's relationship with her children. Keep your criticism to a minimum. And for your daughter's sake, do your best to become the best dad you can be. It will mean learning as much as you can about the needs of young women. In case anyone out there is still wondering, girls are different from boys in more than appearance and apparatus. Girls and boys are physically different, emotionally different, and even spiritually different.

A dad would do well to recognize these things early and get the outside help he needs. Seek the counsel of a few trustworthy women—and *listen* to their advice. Their insights will give you a better understanding and perspective on your girls and their unique needs. Bring the things you learn about women home and apply them wisely.

PHYSICAL DIFFERENCES

My daughter Paige needed practical help when she began her first period. But she also needed to see that her dad cared and that I really did try to meet her needs. I just didn't happen to have any tampons lying around the house to give her. But I could give her personal attention and love.

And speaking of tampons… Stop groaning. Yes, we must talk about tampons. We need to learn the nomenclature and become comfortable talking about it. Let's all say these words together: "Tampon. Bra. Panty liner. Hair clips. Makeup. Feminine hygiene." And that's just for starters. If you have a girl, she needs you to be aware of and open about her personal needs. You won't always be able to help her out, but you need to be available. When my daughter comes to me about feminine itching, I'm pretty limited in the advice I can offer. Yet she knows I love her, so she comes to me about these things. She trusts me enough to talk about anything with me.

I have taken the time to talk to doctors and women I trust, and I've read the backs of boxes and the directions and schematics with regard to feminine hygiene. I still tend to blush when I have to discuss these issues, but it's necessary to talk about them.

Physical differences are easy to identify but equally easy to overlook. Daughters have breasts and a vagina. These differences require certain attention. Fitting a bra is not like fitting a T-shirt. If your daughter's mother is not available, your daughter will need a woman she feels comfortable with to help fit her with the proper bra for support and development.

Your daughter will need someone to discuss health issues with—perhaps an aunt or a woman in the church you trust, maybe a woman who works with the youth group. She will also need a gynecologist. Don't hesitate to find a female doctor who is aware of your single-parenting needs and who cares enough to be involved.

Different women have different schedules and responses to their menstrual cycle. You will need to break the ice in discussing these issues and also locate someone you can call now and then with a question or problem. The nature of their flow and the nature of any other secretions are important issues. Your daughter will need someone she can go to if she feels there is something irregular. While there are many resources for information, children need to be able to come home with all of their most embarrassing and personal issues. Don't trust your children to health class and the misinformation they get from other kids. Your daughter needs you to be open and aware of her changing needs. It's much different than boys, who simply clean their unit (hopefully) and then put it away. I mean, girls can't even see theirs. It's a whole other world. Get smart from the start and don't hide from uncomfortable issues. Treat these matters gently, but don't avoid them. Love your daughter enough to learn.

Personal Appearance

My son Nico comes to the breakfast table two minutes after he wakes up. He's dressed and ready for school. If you brush his hair, it immediately returns to its preferred state of ordered chaos—it's every hair for itself.

We can argue whether it is cultural or innate, but my daughters would never leave the house looking like that. First, their hair is longer, so it requires additional care. Second, aside from tying fishhooks on his head, Nico doesn't want or need any additional decoration. My daughters want braids and ribbons and scrunchies (which I thought was a problem with your underwear) to accentuate their beautiful dome.

Do yourself a favor. Buy a braid book. Go to the hair-care section of a local store and familiarize yourself with the myriad of hair-care products and adornments for tying up one's hair. Go to a school and see what the kids are wearing. Pick up a teen magazine at the bookstore. Looking good is important to girls, and we dads don't totally get it. We tend to downplay these issues too much.

I'm not suggesting you simply follow the crowd or that you allow your daughter to do so. But dads need to be plugged in to a girl's fashion preferences. Part of culture for a young woman is accessorizing. Give them barrettes and bows to experiment with. They will feel glamorous, and they'll be thankful for your efforts to understand.

Nico's idea of personal hygiene is hosing himself down in the yard. Stick him on a cement pad and blow water on him. Get it over with. Young women have different needs. If soap gets near Nico's head, I'm ahead of the game. Young women want hair that is smooth, silky, and smelling good. A bar of soap won't cut it. Shampoo, conditioner, and gels or sprays are a bare minimum. If you want attractive, confident young women, don't tell them to just get over it. Pay close attention to their special needs.

As girls grow up it gets more complicated. Makeup becomes an issue. How much, how little, for what occasions, and at what age? You need to discuss and address these questions. However, you would do well to get some idea what the rest of the planet is doing. It's worth paying someone you trust to give your daughter a makeover. These experts in cosmetics should be able to teach your daughter about colors and seasons and other top-secret appearance intelligence. Paying for a makeover can also be a bonding experience that says to your daughter, "Dad sees that I'm a woman and he approves!"

Clothing Preferences

I went in to wake Nico the other morning. He was naked. He decided clothing was a hassle and ditched every last stitch.

"What are you doing?" I asked.

"Sleepin' nekked."

As I had Nico put his skivvies back on, I marveled at how different it was for my girls. When their mom first moved out, they had nighties and p.j.'s. But I sleep in my underwear, so when their nighties were outgrown, I was oblivious to that development. Oblivious, that is, until I received a call from a friend asking me if I needed some help with my girls.

Paige was spending the night with this woman's daughter and some other girls. I was shocked and even a little scared at the woman's tone when she called. I wondered what tragedy had occurred. What it was, in this instance, was sleepwear. Or the lack of same. I was advised that my daughter didn't have any nighties and was embarrassed to wear my old T-shirt as a nightshirt. The mother on the telephone explained that girls like to dress up even to go to sleep. I fought back my embarrassment and realized I couldn't know all there was to know about raising girls. Sure, give me some help.

The mom offered to take my daughter shopping. She found p.j.'s and nighties and underthings and other stuff that I would have thought absolutely unnecessary. I saw the radiance in my young daughter's smile when she first sat in her nightie and played with all the girl stuff.

This same friend gave me a list of suggested items for face cleaning and skin softening. There are astringents, polish removers, powders, cotton balls, and countless sundries that make up the formula for "sugar and spice and everything nice." I slowly worked these items into the family budget.

Many dads will experience a certain tension as they get up to speed on girls' current fashions. While teen magazines can give you a clue about how teenage girls are dressing and fixing their hair, remember that the clothing styles generally are guided by Hollywood flash. A typical teen magazine won't give modesty a lot of play. You'll see plenty of navel-ringed models dressed in midriff-baring tops, with ample cleavage exposed and lots of leg. But remember, Dad, we're talking about your girl, not some professional model. So remember to emphasize modesty and true beauty, not trendiness.

When girls wear these clothes, they aren't doing themselves any favors. Britney, Madonna, and Christina are entertainers selling an image and influencing fashion trends. However, they're not selling the image I want for *my* girls. It's a dad's responsibility to teach and insist on appropriate boundaries for modest dress. It's not always easy, but remember the need for occasional tough love and learn the art of compromise. Be tough when it matters and flexible when necessary. Remember my daughter's blue hair? Better a daughter with blue hair than a daughter at a swimming party in a thong bikini.

As you keep an eye on modest dress and the reasonable use of makeup, keep in mind the more important issues of building a healthy self-image and keying in on inner beauty. Kindness, loyalty, love, patience, generosity, and other virtues that seek the best for us and for those around us are far more important issues than eyelashes and footwear. As the dad, you need to model these values in your own life if you expect your daughters to adopt these same values for themselves. Remind your girls that what makes them beautiful is who they are, not what they look like. After all, God is looking at the heart.[1]

EMOTIONAL DIFFERENCES

Girls process things differently in the emotional realm. I'm certain that much of this is cultural, but part of it is innate. For instance, you can't expect girls to respond the same way as boys in mixed company. Whether a girl is naturally gentle or not, she wants to be perceived as such just as much as boys desire to be seen as tough. So foster your daughter's gentle spirit. Be careful what you and your son do in front of your daughter. When my sons and I start with the gross comments at the dinner table, for instance, it doesn't take long to see that my daughters are genuinely uncomfortable. They may be just as crude when they are in the company of other girls, but in mixed company they want dads and brothers to respect their sensitivities.

When it comes to emotional makeup and reactions, young women are everything you are not. Don't expect them to act or react as you would. Girls generally need a different type of support system before they will step up and take charge. Young women are typically sensitive, gentle, and less aggressive. They thrive on security and will go out of their way to avoid upsetting the applecart. Boys are bolder and take the risk because their egos enable them to live in denial of ever getting caught. So cater to your daughter's nature. Give her sound paternal support and guard her sensitivities.

My older daughter, Jennifer, is the most aggressive athlete in my family. She hates losing to anyone—male or female. Yet despite all that, she is a woman. She wants her brothers and me to respect her femininity. She will destroy me in a footrace, then turn right around and build me up as the stronger person. Emotionally she needs to feel confident and competent, but she also needs the security of my paternal position. Jennifer is a leader among women and has the gifts and abilities to lead men. Yet something in her wants the approval of her dad.

Therefore, be an active, present father for your girls. Too many girls grow up and marry a man who becomes a father figure. If a girl has her father's focused attention and steady involvement, she will more confidently seek a mate who is a true partner and not a substitute parent.

Be ready for emotional responses by young girls that may confuse you and recognize that logic is not the solution to every problem. When emotional outbursts occur, keep your mouth shut and enjoy the ride. See that your daughter is eating balanced meals, check the calendar, and be a good sounding board. Emotions and hormones are part of the chemistry of being a young woman. Young men have hormones too, but their response is totally different. Instead of falling apart, they fight. It's a testosterone thang. We'll get to that in the next chapter.

As you consider the emotional differences between daughters and sons, give serious thought to a girl's needs in the area of security. We all like the feeling of comfort and security, but this may be more pronounced with your daughter. My sons responded to the reality of divorce with some generalized anger toward women. Meanwhile, my daughters suffered some anger toward their mom. But they faced a different long-range issue—a specific *fear*. Both of my girls are afraid of failure in their relationships. My older daughter is especially fearful of making wrong choices in a romantic relationship, similar to what her mom might have made. *If Mom thought she loved you and was wrong, how do I know if I am really in love?* Jennifer has wondered.

This is a tough question, and I don't have a good answer. I encourage my daughter to trust her judgment and to be prayerful, asking God to lead her to the right man. I remind her that having experienced the tragedy of divorce in her own family, she now understands the potential pitfalls and perils of marriage. Therefore, as she someday approaches marriage, she'll be well aware of the possible outcomes and much better prepared to make a bedrock commitment to her husband. I remind her that anyone can run aground emotionally in a relationship. Before she's married, she still has the freedom to break off from an unwise relationship. Prior to taking the sacred vows, there's no binding commitment she has to honor. No daughter (or son, for that matter) should feel obligated to remain committed to a nonmarital relationship if things have gone awry. It's far better to break it off before the commitment of marriage is made. But once she's married, everything changes.

Don't feel that because your own marriage fell apart that you can't insist on better for your children. I have told my daughter that before she gets married, she must decide for certain that she will never let go, no matter what. Quitting can't be an option. If she takes that option into the marriage relationship, she will weaken a structure that is already guaranteed to suffer tremendous wear and tear over the years. Couples who succeed in marriage attribute their success to two constants—hard work and the commitment to not give up.

Try to work through the fears with your daughter. Help any serious suitors to also understand those fears and recognize the potential liabilities.

SPIRITUAL DIFFERENCES

Just as girls are different in their physical and emotional makeup, they also are unique in their spiritual lives. Males and females express their spirituality differently. To understand this difference, enlist the aid of your spiritual support group's most trusted women. If your daughter's mother is not available or isn't a committed Christian, your daughter might benefit greatly from having a spiritual mentor. But if a woman does take your daughter under her wing, make certain you know what is being taught and keep a close watch on your daughter's spiritual outlook.

I made the mistake of trusting my daughter Paige with a woman who meant well but led Paige in a direction that I considered unhealthy. Paige was part of a worship dance troupe. Slowly and unwittingly, the head of the dance troupe was leading these young girls into a legalistic allegiance to her teachings and behavioral demands. At first glance everything was peachy. Good spiritual teachings were at the core of the woman's presentation. However, she began demanding fanatical adherence to the policies she laid down. Her teachings gradually became more judgmental. I failed to monitor the situation closely because I assumed the woman would uphold sound biblical teaching and because I needed help.

But once I began to get involved, I found a serious imbalance in the teaching my daughter was receiving. It took many talks and much biblical teaching and reading with my daughter to get her back on a balanced path.

"Train a child in the way he should go."[2] Don't abandon your responsibility to teach your daughters what will make them godly women. Look into age-appropriate Bible study aids for girls, then stand in the gap for your young women.

Regard Your Daughters with Understanding

Because boys and girls are different, you must treat your sons and daughters differently. That advice might sound like simple common sense, and it is. But in the busyness of raising our kids, we often forget that our daughters have special needs. If your son asks "How come you spend so much money on all that feminine junk and won't buy me a new cartridge for my GameBoy?" tell him that fair is not always equal and that you love all of your children the same.

If two patients went to the doctor, one with a broken arm and the other with a headache, and the doctor gave each of them two aspirin, that would be the same but hardly what was needed. The nature of the need determines the nature of the response. Let your kids know that fair means doing what is right for the individual child.

When my girls went to their first dance, I gave them something special to wear in their hair to help them feel more attractive. I took pictures. When they got home, there was a special rose on their pillow in their favorite color to remind them that Daddy loved them.

When my older son went to his first dance, I gave him a corsage to give to his date. I gave him a few dollars to carry for confidence. When he got home, we talked all about the girls and the band.

Was I being fair? I don't know. I was being a dad.

Survival Tips

Don't Miss the Milestones

Below is a list of significant milestones in the life of a daughter and some suggested responses from her dad. There is extra space left for you to use in developing more personal responses that fit you and your daughter.

- *First Bra.* Give her a note reminding her that she will always be your special little girl and that you are proud that she is growing up to be such a special woman.

- *Starting Her Menstrual Cycle.* There are a variety of gift books available that commemorate a young girl's passage into womanhood. (With my daughter Paige, I used the book *Butterfly Kisses* by Bob Carlisle.) Also, a certificate or absti- nence ring your daughter can use to dedicate herself to keeping chaste before God is appropriate.[3] Leave a rose on her pillow (pick a color and make it "yours and hers" and use that color for all special occasions) and, as always, find an appropriate greeting card with a special message.

- *First Date.* Give her a corsage and/or an accessory to wear with her outfit, and leave a long-stemmed rose on her pillow for when she returns.

- *First Dance.* Give her an accessory to wear with her dress and/or flowers for her room, turn down her bed, and leave a long-stemmed rose and/or chocolate mint on her pillow, along with a note telling her you love her.

- *First Boyfriend.* Give her a picture frame and a disposable camera.

- *Senior Prom.* Leave a long-stemmed rose on her pillow, and give her a disposable camera.
- *Graduation.* She'll want a car, but see if you can get away with a rose and a card of congratulations, a ring commemorating the event, a name bracelet or anklet, and possibly a special trip with a girlfriend.
- *Leaving for College.* Give her a long-stemmed rose and something special to use in her dorm room, like a throw rug, a new bathrobe, her own embroidered towel, or a set of sheets.
- *First Apartment.* Give her a new microwave, toaster, set of dishes and glasses, flatware, a set of towels, or furniture.
- *Engagement.* Give her a long-stemmed rose. Take the happy couple to dinner.
- *Wedding.* She'll tell you *exactly* what you need to do and what you need to spend. Plan on kissing not only your daughter good-bye but also a good chunk of your savings!

You and Your Son

How to Identify the Special Things Boys Need

HAVING CONSIDERED the challenges dads face in raising girls, you're probably thinking, *Sons, no sweat! We're all guys, after all.*

Think again. Raising boys as a single dad requires just as much care and attention to a child's special needs as does raising girls. You are your son's primary role model. Young boys become young men, and young men reflect their dads. As my dad, Fred Klumpp—noted philosopher and father of three sons—used to mumble, "Apples don't fall far from the tree." Your emotions, passions, and character will be reflected somewhere within the lives of the sons you are raising.

This is really cool, I know. A junior version of you growing into a young man, going out to do good and solve the world's problems. But if we're completely honest with ourselves, we have to also acknowledge the downside—our less-than-stellar traits. Our sons don't pick and choose: They reflect our vices as well as our virtues. With that in mind, we need to borrow some wisdom from the Eighty-second Airborne: It's essential that we recognize our weaknesses.

We're men. We're strong and fearless. We're loud and we're proud. And, oh yeah, we have a few deficiencies. As I write this, there are three males and two females in my home. If the boys and I decide we're angry, there's enough testosterone in the room to drug a racehorse. Not only is that a combustible combination when the males in the family begin to feed off one another's emotions, but it's enough to drive the women in the room to either tears or a tantrum. So watch the slow burn of emotions; they affect not just you but also your entire family.

The Absent Mom

After a divorce, your son's recovery will reflect your own recovery. If you are angry, he will be angry. If you are forgiving, in time he will also forgive.

The first issue I encountered with my sons was their terrible loneliness after their mom left. Immediately, both my six-year-old and my thirteen-year-old felt the emptiness. Each of my sons needed their mom in personal ways. First and foremost, they needed the nurture and feminine touch she brought. This highlights again the need for dads to work overtime on the nurturing issue. The boys' missing their mom was understandable, but what it led to was utterly confusing.

My sons acted out their loneliness in a number of ways. Looking back, I see that part of their reaction was just like mine. In my own way,

I was panicking at the reality of having been rejected by the woman who had promised to love me for life. To try to dull the pain of rejection and loneliness, I found myself latching on to various available women. I was working in a theater as the resident artistic director. There was a pool of available women, and at first I was constantly seeking their attention. I would go out after rehearsal for coffee, invite them to dinner, meet them in the evening—anything to have some female company.

Ron, a good friend and a single dad whose wife left him a few years prior to my own divorce, came to my rescue. He told me to stop experimenting with any new romantic relationships. Once my panic eased up, I took his advice and started concentrating on taking care of my responsibilities at home. But by that time I had left a string of confused and hurt women in my wake, all of them angry with me and some of them way too young for me. I had been acting like a kid instead of being the man my boys needed me to be.

Ron had been through the same thing, and he had survived. He taught me the good things he had learned, and I was willing to implement them in my own life. Though Ron had his daughters only every other weekend and on holidays, he had managed to keep the perspective that *dads need to be dads*—not romance-starved guys out playing the field.

In fact, Dad needs to be Dad all the more as the family heals. I needed to be home in order to assure my children that the ship was not going to sink and there was a responsible person at the helm. I wanted to emulate Ron, who would stay home even when his daughters were with their mom. He wanted to be there just in case his kids needed to call and hear his voice, just in case they wanted the reassurance that Dad loved them and was there for them, even if at a distance.

THE NEED FOR ATTENTION

As noted earlier, boys follow their dads both for good and for ill. My sons, struggling with their loneliness, followed my lead and latched onto their own surrogates. For my younger son, it was his teacher. He sought her attention and approval. Eventually, his need for attention became overwhelming for both him and his overburdened teacher. Five years later, I'm still helping him not to burden his teachers with his own needs.

The teachers were gracious. They loved Nico, guided him, and taught him. If half of their students came from single-parent homes, imagine the load these teachers were carrying. So, Dad, send your child's teacher a thank-you note. And schedule a meeting with her (or him) to learn more about your child. Bite your tongue and take seriously what the teacher has been observing. This feedback is extremely valuable for self-evaluation and also for identifying needs in the lives of your children. Your boys may not act out in your presence, but they will at school. Your child's teacher will be able to help you spot many of your sons' special needs.

A son needs to balance his need for female approval with the reality of his mom being absent or, at the very least, less available than she was before. I encouraged Nico to call his mom anytime, day or night. (This is another reason not to denigrate your ex-wife in front of your kids. They *need* their mom.) In addition, I had several discussions with Nico in front of his teachers to say that we understood his need for their approval. We told him outright that it was because he was trying to fill the gap left by his mom. Then we encouraged him to seek his teacher's approval by applying himself to his schoolwork and not by coming to the teacher's desk with questions to get her attention. The teachers always added, without prompting, "Nico, you know I love you." And they meant it.

So the teacher would feel free to express affection in a way that was comfortable for her and for Nico, I gave her my permission to give my son a touch or hug if she felt it appropriate. In today's world of lawsuits and sexual confusion, many teachers understandably choose not to show any physical attention to a student. (In fact, in many school districts, teachers are instructed *not* to touch students in any way.) Nico needed safe female touch. For me, a first-grade teacher's shoulder squeeze seemed like a good compromise. On the other hand, if my older son (a teenager) were to come home with his teacher's perfume on his shirt, I'd start worrying. I'd never allow any of my children to ride alone in a car with a teacher or to go off campus with a teacher unchaperoned. This is not safe for your child or for the teacher. Take Robert Frost's advice: "Good fences make good neighbors."[1] Provide appropriate boundaries to protect your son as well as the significant women in his life.

Write down the names and roles of the significant females in the lives of your sons, then go see them. This would include neighborhood moms, teachers, Boy Scout volunteers, and youth workers at church. Seek their assistance in monitoring and helping your sons. I asked the mom of my younger son's good friend to help me out. To Nico and me, she is forever John Bill's mom.[2] Nico's friend John Bill (a boy bearing a good, Texas two-name moniker) attended the same church we did. They lived around the corner within safe walking distance. Nico was prone to stop by their house on the way home from school on the pretense of visiting John Bill. Of course, with every visit he would seek out a hug from John Bill's mom. Along with cookies and milk, those hugs were a gift from God. If your son doesn't have a safe, caring woman around like John Bill's mom, find one.

An Older Son's Needs

My older son, Ian, was thirteen when his mom left, and his panic was much closer to my own. He would react to every woman who visited our home, even those who were nothing more than casual friends. He was so eager to have a woman in our family that he would seek the woman's attention and draw close to her children. This pattern became the biggest motivation for me to get my dating behavior under control. I saw my panic reflected in my older son, and I sensed that he was competing for the attentions of some of the women I was trying to date. I wised up and stopped dating for a long time. I kept female friends—at least those in whom I had some romantic interest—at a distance and away from my children. Once I had made that decision, my older son's emotions and panic subsided.

Still, a thirteen-year-old boy is capable of forming his own female relationships. I felt Ian was too young to date, but schoolyard romances happen whether dating happens or not. It was time to level with my son.

Ian and I frequently went out to do things together. While we were out, I made certain to bring up the issue of his feelings toward girls and women, and I used myself as both a good and a bad example. I explained my panic. I talked about overcompensating to fill the need that we both had for a woman's attention. I encouraged him to be careful in his relationships with girls. I always asked him who he liked and kept my ears open to learn about his current crush.

When listening to your son, it's important to not interrupt; just allow him to express himself fully. Jumping in too quickly with advice about relationships is usually not well received. Make mental notes and give the advice at a later time when you're not supposed to be just listening. Besides, you're recovering from a divorce. Maybe your advice needs some scrutiny before you lay it on your son. Maintain credibility by being honest with your boys about your own failures. The know-it-all-dad routine ain't gonna work, especially if you recently crashed and burned. So be supportive and listen carefully. Take notes, if you need to, and respond at another special moment.

With Ian, the main thing we needed to establish was respect toward girls and women. Respect has real meaning for Ian because of his martial-arts training, which demands that each student respect both himself and his opponent as well as his teacher. In martial arts, the rules of engagement govern what can and cannot be done during competition. Likewise, Ian knew that respecting women meant respecting clear and necessary boundaries. We decided to work on this together by exercising balance and honesty. I listened to him not only when he told me about his relationships, but also when he gave advice about my own. It took time, but I learned to listen and share, and we both gained wisdom in the way we sought out feminine attention.

Dealing with Anger

Anger is a secondary emotion, usually an outward response to the emotional pain we are experiencing. With my divorce, I expected anger and there was some. However, the greater anger came years later. It was a slow-burning anger. Anger was an issue for my sons as well. If your wife is gone, your sons will be angry with women. So be on the lookout.

For Ian, my older son, it came more quickly than with Nico. Ian expressed some immediate anger. This was obvious enough and easy to deal with. The more subtle issues of anger were expressed over time and at first were acted out with Ian's sisters.

There is such a thing as having too much "man" in a home. You know you've reached that point when your home begins to look like a hunting lodge or a frat house. We'll talk more about that later. But it's also easy to have too much man attitude in a home. Though I've never been a macho-rights antifeminist, in my own hurt over the divorce I began noticing some unhealthy "men are the stronger sex" comments rolling out of my mouth. Remarks about a woman's self-centeredness or women being emotional rather than rational are harmful enough when offered flippantly in a healthy environment. When there are bruised emotions after a divorce, these same statements can leave lasting scars on the children who are listening to Dad run off at the mouth.

I came unglued one night as I watched election returns and heard a comment about Hillary Clinton perhaps being a good candidate for the first female president. I slandered all womankind as I remarked on "female qualities" that made a woman ill-equipped to run the military during a national or international crisis. As I think back on it, phrases such as "too compassionate" and "afraid to act forcefully" ring a bell. I had to go back and apologize to Ian as I realized he was drinking in every destructive word.

To make matters worse, Nico was shattered. His military hero of all heroes was Joan of Arc. Had I destroyed his respect for this brave woman? I was relieved recently when I read a sixth-grade history paper that Nico had written in which he stated that the figure in history he would most like to be is Joan. I guess he forgave my ignorance.

In the meantime, let me revisit Fred Klumpp's immortal wisdom about apples and trees. My son Ian heard every lame-brained comment I made about women, and he quickly became the poster boy for a new organization, Men Against Equal Rights for Women. His audience was his two sisters, and his goal was to get under their skin by making preposterous comments. He'd voice a chauvinistic sentiment, such as "Women belong in the kitchen, so, Jennifer, get in the kitchen and make me some lunch!" This was especially absurd considering I've always been the parent who did the most work in the kitchen. And partially masking Ian's anger were his lame attempts to make these declarations sound like humor.

Jennifer, Ian's older sister, would ignore him or just tell him where to get off. But Paige, my younger daughter, would walk right into the trap. She could never escape Ian's theater of the absurd without hurt feelings coupled with raised voices and a lot of anger.

Ian was acting out some real hurt and disappointment that stemmed from his mother's leaving, and he was directing that anger toward his sisters. He seemed to feel a need to punish his sisters simply because they were female.

This was unfair to my daughters, of course, but if I rushed in to stop Ian altogether, I would be sending the message that his feelings were invalid. If I didn't stop him, on the other hand, his sisters would feel that I agreed with Ian that women were inferior. I chose a middle ground and corrected Ian in front of his sisters. I acknowledged that his hurts had probably left him feeling some anger toward women and that I could see he was directing that anger toward his sisters. I made it clear I understood his anger and hurt. Then I pointed out that hurtful comments were not going to bring healing to his own hurt. He would typically respond that he was just pushing his sisters. Rather than try to convince him I was right, I simply left it there and went on, knowing I'd made my point.

In addition to discussing these matters in front of my daughters, I also regularly went into Ian's room later and asked, "Son, do you really feel that way about women?" Then he would usually shoot straight, and

I could remind him to show more respect when talking in front of his sisters. I would also confess to Ian my own guilt in making similar negative comments, so he'd know I understood his feelings. Over time, my son's unwarranted comments dissipated.

As Ian has grown, I've had several checkpoints at which I question him on his feelings about girls. The questions are usually subtle. "How's it going with the girl you're dating?" Then I listen not only to his answer but also to the tone and the subtleties behind his answer. Bottom line: He seems to have developed a healthy respect for women as people. Keeping the communication open and honest has been invaluable.

The Need to Tone Down "Animal House"

Is there such a thing as too much man? You betcha! Any home that is inhabited by both sons and daughters can become a place with too much man. What do I mean by that? Well, I myself knocked down a wall in my house and created Café Klumpp, complete with twinkle lights and a sound stage so my musician friends could come by and play their music. In fact, given the chance and without the balance of feminine tastes, I would quite likely have re-created Animal House right in my own house. In short, my home needed the touches of domestic comfort—not the atmosphere of a nightclub. It needed a balancing feminine touch.

One night, at about midnight, I yanked Ian out of bed. We drove to a nearby river, where we loaded my truck with rocks to decorate our yard. As we drove home, I decided to ignore the driveway and pulled up in the front yard so we could stack the rocks in the shape of a cross. Then I poured some gasoline on the ground and burned the cross in so the grass wouldn't grow up through the rocks. I can still imagine my neighbors looking out their windows, hearing the racket, and saying,

"What in the world are they doing now?" while my daughters hid in their rooms thinking, *Oh no, this can't be happening.*

Some men might prefer a hunting lodge motif or a game arcade in the basement with a pool table, video games, and decorations consisting of street signs and traffic lights. (I'm not suggesting removing these from public property. You can get old ones at a flea market.) One friend built a walk-in humidor in his closet. Not necessarily a bad idea, but he didn't even smoke. He just thought it would be cool to be prepared in case a friend ever wanted to store some cigars.

While these are matters of personal taste and not moral questions, for my own family, I realized that I needed to create a more homelike home. Bohemian is one thing; frat house is another. There is definitely such a thing as too much man.

Your daughters need a place where they will feel comfortable, and your sons need to learn how to be gentlemen. A man's earthiness has a time and a place—such as with other guys on a fishing trip. However, you want your sons to be both men and gentlemen and to know when each is called for. As a single dad, you need to avoid overdoing the macho thing around your sons.

Young men need to know there is a time and a purpose for polite conversation. Certain types of humor, while acceptable with a bunch of guys sitting around a campfire, are clearly off-limits in mixed company. Teach your sons how to reserve manly expressions of opinion and humor for the appropriate time and place. It's important that we show our young men not only how to clean fish and shoot defenseless woodland creatures, but also how to show respect to girls and women in the way we conduct ourselves. Reserve the earthy stuff for times of men-only bonding.

My young men are asked to wear shirts at the dinner table. They are asked to avoid making references to body odors and bodily noises when in mixed company. They are asked to filter their humor through me before going public around the girls. A response of "Yes sir" or "Yes ma'am" when speaking to adults is still considered good manners. We don't lick the plates clean, even when the gravy is superior. We don't drink straight out of the milk jug, and knife throwing is discouraged indoors. You get the idea.

Manners are learned and vary from one culture to the next. But generally, our society acknowledges fairly standard practices that work to keep the male populace from reverting to a pseudobarbaric state. There are good books on manners available at the library, and there are even helpful Web sites dedicated to the fine art of etiquette.[3]

Remember, there are really two issues here. One is the natural tendency for males to rush from order to disorder when they have no females around to balance things out. The other issue is that we have to monitor our reactions to girls and women, reactions that might grow out of our hurt and anger. The push to be male may come as overcompensation for the hurt or rejection we feel we have received from the key woman in our lives. So strive for balance.

THE FEAR OF REJECTION

As your sons grow, keep an eye out for any indicators that signal a fear of rejection. While the divorce may have happened to you, it actually happened to your children as well. In fact, they often think it was their fault. If someone thinks they're on fire, throw water on them, then try to reason with them. As long as they think they're burning, they won't hear what you're trying to tell them. Put out the flames first, then you might have a chance to be heard.

Your children deserve to know the facts. First, it's not their fault. They need to be reassured of this and probably more than once. And while their mom may have left you, emphasize that she didn't leave her children. She loves them even though she decided not to remain married to their father.

Your children's sense of rejection is as great as your own. Yet they are not nearly as well equipped to deal with those feelings simply because they haven't had that many years to develop coping skills. Your sons will carry a fear of rejection somewhere within their psyche, so keep a lookout. It will affect their future relationships if it's not dealt with now. In fact, it may not become evident until it strikes in a relationship. Then you will need to sit down and explain to them how a fear of rejection might color their feelings about the relationship.

Don't invalidate their feelings. They feel what they feel. Instead, explain that their feelings may be saying "Don't get involved" or "Don't let go" when it's actually time to do just the opposite. Let them know that their feelings and their reactions to what they feel may be rooted in a fear of rejection.

For Nico, this fear surfaced in an unhealthy compulsion to please females. He was trying too hard to make a positive impression. He feared their rejection so he tried to win their approval and then confirm it over and over. Sometimes his overeagerness pushed buttons that caused these women to react impatiently. Then Nico's fears were confirmed: "I knew they would eventually stop liking me."

For Ian, the issue has shown itself in other ways. He went through an extended period during which he wasn't happy unless he was being noticed by the opposite sex. Then, once he got into a relationship, he found it difficult to let go—even after the relationship had soured. Over time, with constant affirmation from me and open discussion

YOU AND YOUR SON

about rejection, he regained his confidence and his relationships settled into a more balanced, healthy pattern. When he finally finds his true love, however, Dad will be there to remind him to check his feelings and not forget that he might see some insecurities raise their ugly head. I will be there to remind him to trust his wife, to trust her love for him, and not to overreact or be oppressive in a constant need to be affirmed.

For divorced dads and the children of divorce, the fear of rejection will forever need to be monitored. Healthy self-assessment and an awareness of the potential of the problem will go a long way toward prevention.

So let's recap.

- Mom is absent, so the home has lost her feminizing influence. Dad needs to develop a more nurturing outlook. He may also need to "recruit" a female friend—a teacher, a neighbor, a church youth leader—to add a woman's touch to his son's life.

- Boys will need some extra encouragement and attention to round out the fact that they miss their mom. Be a shoulder to lean on, or cry on, as necessary.

- Watch the older boys. Make certain they behave well with their sisters and with female friends. There may be a tendency to act out their anger. They need to be reminded to keep a respectful attitude toward all girls and all women.

- There is such a thing as having too much man in the home. So keep your hand on the volume knob.

- Help your boys work through their fear of rejection. Give them a platform for building confidence in relationship to girls and women.

Survival Tips

Too Much Man on the Home Front?

This checklist will help you determine if there is too much man in your home:

1. At Christmas, do you and your boys have a contest to see who can shoot the most reindeer decorations in the front yard?

2. Have you replaced all the lights in your house with black light bulbs and strobes?

3. Is a deer's head mounted in the shower?

4. Have you dressed up your living room sofa with a NASCAR throw cover?

5. Is each sofa cushion hiding a whoopee cushion?

6. Have dirty dishes stacked up so high that you wash them with a garden hose in the backyard?

7. Do your place settings consist of paper, plastic, and foam?

8. Have your daughters started wearing helmets to guard against being hit with a football in the house?

9. Does the fifth hole of a Frisbee golf course run through your den?

10. Have you used your chainsaw to cut wood—indoors?

Answer Key

If you answered yes to any of these questions, there is *too much man* in your home! Your daughters don't want to live in Animal House, and your sons need more balance in their lives. So, if you notice too much man at home, you're just going to have to kiss some of that testosterone good-bye.

THE IRREGULAR MATH
OF SINGLE PARENTING

The Needed Twenty-Seven-Hour Day
and Other Things That Don't Add Up

CAN YOU SAY "tired"? A better question is, "Do you have enough energy to say 'tired'?"

While I was writing this chapter, I asked my kids if there was anything they thought I should mention to other single dads.

"Yeah," Nico offered, after giving it some thought. "Tell people not to make peanut-butter-and-ranch-dressing sandwiches for their kids."

"What are you talking about?" I asked. "When did you ever have a peanut-butter-and-ranch-dressing sandwich?"

"You put one in my lunch when we lived in Duncanville."

"No, son, I never put peanut butter and ranch dressing in your lunch. You're just confused about it."

"Yes, you did."

"No, I didn't."

And so the argument went. Of course, I won. No one in his right mind would make his kid a peanut-butter-and-ranch-dressing sandwich, even in a single dad's most experimental mode.

A few days later I was talking to Ian, my older son. "Ian," I asked, "did I ever put anything really strange in your lunch?"

"Not that I remember," he replied.

"Nothing? I mean, nothing you remember from the Duncanville house?"

"No."

"I didn't think so." I'd been exonerated.

"Oh, wait a minute," Ian said. "Yeah, there was one lunch I didn't understand. I had a turkey-and-jelly sandwich. That was kinda weird."

Sleep deprivation and burnout are my only excuses, and of course I had to apologize to Nico for saying he was mistaken about the peanut-butter-and-ranch-dressing sandwich. Once again, I was humbled by the mercy and generosity of my children, who never mentioned a word about the mix-up to me at the time.

MATH FOR SINGLE DADS

No amount of prayer or wishing or complaining will change the fact that, as a single dad, you are destined to run behind in any domestic endeavor you undertake. You need at least twenty-seven hours each day just to settle in at being a *little* behind. The twenty-four-hour day was invented not for single dads but for two resident parents, and the original plan even included eight hours of sleep. You're a single dad, a one-man show, and you're in over your head.

The demands of single fatherhood are exhausting for all of us, and for dads who lean toward perfectionism, the self-imposed demands are even more unreachable. We each have expectations of how a home should operate based on our upbringing, our temperament, or our observations of how other families operate. These are not absolute standards sent down from on high; they are human ideas of how things should work. So stop, take a deep breath, and eliminate the unnecessary pressure. You don't have time for comparisons, especially comparisons that steal your confidence and add stress to your day.

Reject the comparisons so you can concentrate on logistics. You have troops to feed and supplies to transport. To succeed, you'll need the help of some simple math and science. The word *logistics* is a military science term for the mathematics of transportation and supplies and the movement of troops. When discussing the efforts of a single dad, the formula goes something like this: Single dad (sd) plus children on the move (cm) exceeds the limitations of the man-hours in a day (24mH), or sd + cm > 24mH.

Since you need at least three additional hours per day that don't exist, you're going to have to figure out what to *stop* doing. When it all can't get done, it's time to trim what gets attempted. To begin the process of elimination, honestly answer this question: Other than serving God, what is your number-one priority? The things that are most important to you will determine everything else in your life. Your actions demonstrate your true convictions.

If you didn't answer the question above with "my kids," then you need to answer it again—but after doing a little soul-searching. You have a window of only about eighteen years of deliberate parenting with each of your children. The parenting after that is mostly damage control and troubleshooting. During the period of deliberate parenting you need to make your children job number one. Here's the math of my situation. My younger son had just turned six when his mom left. Six from eighteen leaves twelve. Whatever my priorities were before, Nico suddenly needed me to make my family number one for the next twelve years. Someone needed to clothe, feed, transport, teach, encourage, discipline, and offer companionship for Nico until he could strike out on his own. The task fell to me.

I was forty-one when I became a single dad. Forty-one plus twelve equals fifty-three. When I do long-term planning, age fifty-three is when I plan to regain some of the freedom to place my agenda before the daily needs of my children. In the meantime, the family is first.

This takes courage, because it doesn't come naturally to put the welfare of others ahead of personal desires. I used to wonder if I'd ever have the courage to "take a bullet" for someone else. Would I *really* put myself in their place to spare their life?[1] Remember, courage is not the absence of fear. It's an issue of the will, the inner fortitude to keep going despite tremendous odds against a successful outcome. Would I give up my life for my dearest friends? When my wife left, I was given a chance to die for my four most precious friends: Jennifer, Ian, Paige, and Nico. Believe me when I tell you that it takes a daily routine of dying to self to give your family your very best.

To get done the twenty-seven hours' worth of work required every day, you'll have to discard a lot of things, including some activities and projects that you absolutely love. But which do you love more—your kids or your favorite hobby? Much of your life is out of control right now. However, there is one area you *can* control—your decisions and choices about what you will devote yourself to. Give God first place in your life, then focus on your children. You'll still have years of life to devote to personal pursuits after your kids leave the house. Make the most of the time you have with them now.

HEALTHY DIET, ADEQUATE REST

Setting aside the math for a moment, let's talk about physical endurance. To be at your best, you'll have to make time for adequate rest and exercise. You may be so harried that you often skip exercise and shortchange your sleep. With the ridiculous schedule before you, you just keep running and doing and then risk becoming depleted and dying on the inside. Call it burnout or a meltdown, it will cloud your judgment, destroy your emotional well-being, and annihilate your spiritual motivation. So as you look at your schedule, make room for rest and exercise.

In addition, you have to eat right. The body is an energy machine. Feed it the right foods, fuel it well, and the energy burn is pure and ample. Feed it poor-quality fuel and you burn out early. Poor fuels often invite the use of additives. However, most engine additives, whether in your car or in your body, have their own side effects. They burn too hot, scorch cylinders, melt gaskets, and foul plugs. Burning processed sugar or caffeine to energize your system will carry the same destructive side effects.

The necessary routines of proper fueling and adequate rest also work to help your children deal with their own stress. You've seen the negative effects on the poorly fueled family: The kids eat what's handy (not once in a while, but always) and stay up late goofing off, listening to music, watching television, or playing video games. And yet their dad can't understand why his children are so moody and unmotivated. We all need to maintain balance in life, which includes a good diet, exercise, and adequate rest.

It's difficult to train a child's sleep habits, especially if he or she has already established poor habits. But it is doable and necessary. Like any habit, unhealthy sleep patterns will take time to break; then you'll expend more time in training them to develop good sleep habits. Some experts estimate it takes three weeks to break an old habit and another two weeks to establish a new one in its place. If that's true, look forward to at least five weeks of retraining. Set a bedtime and stick to it. Be flexible by allowing some room for quiet bedtime activities such as reading (but not handheld video games). In my home, bedtime is time to get in bed and to get quiet but not necessarily an order to immediately fall asleep.

SANITY IN SCHEDULING

In addition to adequate rest and a healthy diet, mealtime itself is a crucial event for the one-parent family. Most two-parent homes have enough trouble corralling everyone together at the table. So it's understandable that people would cut a single dad some slack if he doesn't consistently get his kids to sit down together for meals. However, the dinner table is an extremely critical issue for the single-parent family, perhaps even more critical than it is for a two-parent home.

Mealtime is a time for community. It's a time for sharing ideas, thoughts, feelings, and the day's events. It is a bonding time. For the single dad, this time of shared community is essential. It builds loyalty and comradeship. It lifts the morale of the troops. So strive to schedule a dinner hour that will bring your family together not only for a good meal, but for much-needed bonding and communication.

Actually, a dinner hour could be the least of your scheduling challenges. To survive as a single dad, you need to employ workable scheduling strategies for family life in general. You go to work every day to support your family, and few dads keep to a strict eight-to-five, Monday-through-Friday week. Many jobs require long days, evenings, or weekends. Some men work the night shift, and others have regular out-of-town travel. With these variables in mind, let's look at the most constant time references in the lives of typical Americans.

The controlling issue for many of us is school. Classes generally begin between 7:30 and 8:00 in the morning and end between 2:00 and 3:00 in the afternoon. Kids have to go to school and parents are responsible for getting them there. So a school's start time and end time will impose themselves on your family's schedule—including your own.

To help you sketch out a grid to establish your family schedule, I'll use a school day of 8:00 to 3:00 as an example. And I'll assume two other daily events that are fairly static in our culture: breakfast and dinner. My family eats breakfast at about 7:00 A.M. on school days, and we usually eat dinner at about 7:00 P.M. I have four kids, and three are athletes, so dinner is often shifted to accommodate their after-school activities.

To get started on creating a sane family schedule, get out a calendar. I use a homemade facsimile of a large desk calendar—a thirty-nine-cent piece of poster board with my own hand-drawn calendar on it. With a marker in one hand and the calendar in front of you, get a semester's worth of organization done if you can. Then update your calendar on a weekly basis.

Gather your kids for a family meeting. Such a gathering will bring unity and give everyone a voice. Pencil in everyone's schedule and special events on the family calendar. The objective becomes one of working inside these schedules and special events to deliver as many meals together as possible. If you can all be together for dinner three or four times a week, you're doing great.

Set a dinner hour that will maximize the chances of everyone's being present. Then let this be a constant, the anchor for your family routine. With the chaos that is added to family life after a divorce, your kids need the stability of a consistent dinner hour when everyone can reconnect.

Basic Menu Planning

For the sake of discussion, let's establish a dinnertime of 7:00 P.M. You'll need to be in the kitchen around 6:00 for meal preparation. Understand, though, this is not the time to decide your menu; you'll need to determine the meal plan in advance.

Many dads cringe at the thought of meal preparation. (See chapter 9 for plenty of handy recipes.) It helps to remember that children's palates are quite forgiving. They're not looking for châteaubriand. Fish sticks and macaroni with cheese is just as good—as long as you balance these with healthy essentials such as fresh fruit and veggies.

To ease the pressure of menu planning, most dads will benefit from planning a week's worth of meals at one time. Plan the menu, then shop to obtain the needed ingredients. Keep your menus simple. A tuna-salad sandwich with carrot sticks and sliced apple is nourishing and easy to prepare. It is also enough for most children. The warmth of sitting together around the table makes up for the occasional lack of a hot meal.

For menu planning, consider relying on a general selection of simple main courses. Add fruits and vegetables to complement these main course ideas.

- Monday: spaghetti and meat sauce or fish sticks with macaroni and cheese
- Tuesday: hot dogs and chips or soup and salad
- Wednesday: pot roast or stewed chicken with fresh vegetables (easy to prepare in the slow cooker while you're at work)
- Thursday: Sloppy Joes (good with lean ground turkey) with carrot sticks and apple sauce
- Friday: varies
- Saturday: varies
- Sunday: grilled hamburgers and fries (for variety, try using sweet potatoes for the fries)

You may prefer more detail and, in fact, you may need a detailed list when you shop. I buy certain things on autopilot. Staples include sandwich meat, spaghetti noodles, spaghetti sauce, tomato sauce, lettuce, tomatoes, bananas, apples, peanut butter, jelly, celery, carrots, onions, mayonnaise, ketchup, potatoes, frozen fries, canned tuna, and ground meat. The rest of what I assemble is based primarily on my budget and a few easy, quick meal ideas. It's tougher to shop when your budget is slim, but with the items above I know I can get through.

Take a look at what you like to eat. You will likely take more interest in preparing what you enjoy. Meals may get to be repetitious over the months. Don't sweat it. Those routine meals will become the fodder for laughter in the future when your children look back. For instance, I love pasta and can prepare it several different ways. The kids eat it because they're hungry, and they laugh because it's "Dad food." My kids tell me their hearts always sink when they see me filling the big pot with water. "Arrggghhhh! Run! It's gonna be spaghetti again!"

GET A GRIP ON THE MORNING RUSH

With dinnertime as an evening anchor and your family calendar beginning to bring some sanity to your family's schedule, you can now organize the other pivotal times of your day. It's time to get on top of morning chaos.

For the sake of discussion, we'll assume you need to be out the door by 7:00 A.M. Use this as your starting point for the rest of the day's schedule. If you can shower, shave, and dress in ten minutes and your children follow suit, your wake-up time might be 6:00 A.M. But bear in mind that all sorts of things crop up unexpectedly. If you prepare everyone's lunch the night before, you'll buy yourself some time. But if you need more than ten minutes to get showered and dressed, and if you like a hot breakfast and reading the paper, you're back to a 5:30 A.M. start time. Make some choices in advance so that the occasional crises don't derail your morning.

Since sleep is a habit, maintain a consistent wake-up time and have your kids do the same. If you let them hit the snooze button, it will become a habit. If you get them on their feet promptly at the same time every morning, this becomes their habit.

When I entered the single-dad life, my kids weren't motivated to get up for school. I had to work up a schedule and then work on the kids to get them moving. Part of what motivated the process was my impatience. Too much patience, and there is no urgency to get the day started.

The first step is deciding what time you will leave the house. Then back up to the time necessary to get rolling and allow a few minutes extra for dragging rear ends. Let's say you need all the kids to hit the deck at 6:00 A.M. Make your initial call at 5:55: "Time to get up." At

6:00, make your second pass. If they are up, give them a destination: "Breakfast in fifteen minutes" or "Get in the shower and get out. Your sister is waiting." If they are still snoozing, pull the covers off and say, "Let's go. Get dressed. You've got ten minutes."

Giving the children goals in ten- or fifteen-minute increments is critical. It plans time and structure in their minds. With a goal there is a need to move. Without a goal, the default mode is "Ahhh, a few more minutes in the sack won't hurt." What does Proverbs say? "A little sleep, a little slumber…and poverty will come on you like a bandit."[2] Hit the snooze one time too many and you're late. So get them up and give them a deadline and a clear destination. Once you do this, the next issue is accountability. Keep them on track.

Caution: Don't do it for them! If they just won't get it going, develop some type of consequence: "Miss the bus, you walk." "Not up by second call, cold water on the feet." "Make me late for work, and you'll be late for something you really want to do later on." Punishments are not fun. That's the point. But punishments should always be fair, swift, and always in proportion to the offense.

LEARN THE LAUNDRY SHUFFLE

Schedules are one thing; basic needs—such as clean clothes—are another. No one wants to go to school or show up for work in smelly clothes, and no one wants to have to live with the clutter of piles of laundry. So it's time to learn a new dance step—the laundry shuffle. This system works even for me, a big-picture kind of guy—which is not an asset when it comes to laundering clothes.

With four children there is an ever-growing pile of laundry in my home. I have tried to regulate the flow through bath-towel management and suggestions on wearing jeans and shirts more than once before they return to the clothes hamper. But try as I might, the laundry pile wins and I lose every time. Which points to the need for learning the laundry shuffle. It's my only hope for survival. Here are the dance steps: Every time one of us goes through the kitchen, we stop at the washer and dryer and do the shuffle. Clothes on the floor are divided into whites and colors. What's in the dryer goes to the couch. What's in the washer is moved to the dryer, and what's on the floor goes into the washer. Turn on the washer and dryer, then shuffle off.

We constantly shuffle the laundry in this routine. The task is everyone's chore. We all like to wear clean clothes (with the exception of Nico, who couldn't care less), so we all pitch in. I manage the greater volume of wash as long as I have kids folding clothes before they sit on the couch or while they talk on the phone or watch television.

And speaking of chores: We try to get most of our household tasks done without resorting to a chore list. I prefer a total-responsibility model that goes like this: If you see something that needs to be done, go ahead and do it. Don't compare what you're doing to what someone else is doing. The doing is its own reward.

This requires management and attention in order to ensure that one child is not doing all the work while the others take a free ride. However, the responsibility model builds a team spirit and family unity, with each person pitching in so that the family as a whole succeeds.

Each child's room is his or her own responsibility. Common areas are community responsibilities. If a glass is left on a table, forget who left it there. Just go ahead and pick it up. Over time, if someone sets down a glass or ice-cream dish and begins to walk away, someone else will almost always issue an alert: "Nico, come back here and carry your dishes to the sink." It's a process of teamwork and team accountability.

We have tried to dispense with blame and finger-pointing and instead promote a proactive lifestyle.

This system has been a real boon to my family. Find what works for yours. If you find these models helpful as a beginning point, tweak them to make them uniquely your own.

In martial-arts instruction, I have learned that the sweeping high kick that works for some stylists won't work for me. I am short and round, not long and graceful. I'm much better suited to quick and powerful. So I teach my karate students to find what works for them. I teach some basic techniques, then hope that they begin a journey of self-discovery.

You should do the same in the journey of single parenting. Discover what works for you in accomplishing what needs to get done each day: planning menus, setting schedules, doing chores. Find satisfaction in knowing that you are struggling along a difficult path that many would fear to even attempt. It's a marathon, and you run it one step at a time. In years to come, your kids will thank you for staying in the race until you all cross the finish line.

Survival Tips

Getting Organized on the Cheap

After years of struggling to devise a workable time-management system, my brother and I landed on the Yellow Pad Management System. It takes some time to get things set up in the beginning. But once you're accustomed to it, it will save you hours and will also go a long way toward getting you and your family organized.

Collect a standard or legal-size pad, a small calendar, an address book (optional), and a pen or pencil. Now let the genius of simplicity revolutionize your life.

Take your pad and write today's date at the top. In addition, I use the upper margin to write down an encouraging reminder that will help me throughout the day. Often it's a Bible verse, such as "I can do all things through Him who strengthens me"[3] or "Be strong and courageous."[4] Other times it's a simple motivating thought, such as "Think thin, be thin." Whatever I need to be reminded of, that's what I write down. In addition, if you have created a mission statement or list of personal goals, keep them visible in your time organizer as a daily reminder of your long-range destination.

Down the left-hand margin write out the hours of your day. Start with the time of day when you first need to record an appointment or event that needs your attention. Then number each hour to the end of your day. Down the center of your page, draw a line from top to bottom. In the left-hand column, using your calendar as a reference, mark any appointments at the appropriate time. In the gaps organize your other meetings or obligations. The left half of your page will be filled with the day's activities, hour by hour.

At the top of the page, to the right of the vertical line, write *To Do*. In that quadrant, list the things you need or want to get done that day. To help organize your list, prioritize the activities with a numbering system. The number one slot represents the things that *must* be done that day. Number two includes the things that need to be done soon but are not urgent. The number three position includes things that are important but can wait for later in the week. If you want to designate a particular time in your day to meet one of these needs, put it in a time slot to the left, where you have your day's hourly schedule.

Halfway down the page on the right-hand side, draw a horizontal line from the center line to the right edge of the page. Above that line write *Notes* or *Expenses* or *Prayer*, whatever does the most to help you stay organized. Then use the lower-right quadrant to fill in items that fit your system. You can also use this space to detail helpful management needs, such as grocery lists, meal plans, mileage, phone numbers, and addresses. You are inventing your own schedule page, so adapt it to fit your needs.

Set a regular time at the beginning or end of each day to create the next day's schedule. As long-range appointments come about, reference them to your calendar. If you wrote down a new address or phone number, transfer it to your address book. You can keep a running log of past activities simply by keeping the old pages attached to the legal pad. When you go to set up your new day, refer to the previous page and carry over items that didn't get done or need to be rescheduled.

Okay, it ain't fancy, but it's easy to adapt the system to make it

(continued)

work for you. If you need to do a week at a glance, do it. You can also use two pages per day, which will give you additional room to add other matters that call for good organization, such as dinner menus, a shopping list, birthdays, and other special occasions. The important thing is just to do it.[5]

7

BASIC STRATEGIES FOR DAILY SUCCESS

Grab More Life with a Lot Less Hassle

LAST NIGHT I WAS reminded that just when you think you have things running somewhat smoothly, you still can't relax.

Here's what happened. My younger daughter was saying something about needing to talk with her older sister. She didn't technically tell me this. Instead, she was using a tone I think of as "I am talking to myself so you can hear and come to my rescue." Of course, I did my best to come to her rescue. And that's where things got dicey.

When I asked Paige why she needed her sister, she shyly declined to tell me. This gesture means there is a need for more discretion since brothers were present. That also told me that whatever was brewing was not going to be fun. It would doubtless fall in the feminine world of a yeast infection or matters of personal hygiene.

My daughter and I moved to the secret recesses of our back hallway. I learned there would be a swimming party and it would collide with a certain time of the month. Then I learned that you can't swim with pads. You need a tampon. (I may be dense, but I'm not unwilling to learn.) It follows, then, that if you need a tampon you need to know how to apply it. But the little graphic in the box was missing.

My daughter was upset about not knowing how and embarrassed at having to bring this up with her dad. (Thankfully, I had an older daughter who could step in later.) The lesson here is that dads need to be extremely patient and willing to keep growing with each new, uncomfortable opportunity. Don't lose heart. You will be the tallest man alive if you just keep growing.

These opportunities for growth present themselves with maddening regularity. They are part of the terrain of the single-dad enterprise. To stay on top of things, you'll need to practice a few simple keys to success. Three areas in particular require your special attention. Those areas are how to maximize your time, how to succeed on limited finances, and what to do with your anger. Any one of these challenges on its own could turn you into a mumbling, drooling lunatic. All three together can totally derail your life. So get started working on some strategies for success in each area.

Make the Most of an Insane Schedule

Time puts us all on an equal footing. We vary in skills and talent and intelligence. But every person on the planet has twenty-four hours every day. So a bigger question than "How much time do we have?" is "How do we use the time that we have?"

At the end of *Moby Dick,* author Herman Melville said it this way: "Now small fowls flew screaming over the yet yawning gulf, a sullen white surf beat against its steep sides; then all collapsed, and the great shroud of the sea rolled on as it rolled five thousand years ago."[1] When we're dead and gone, the earth will go on as it has in the past. So while you still have breath, make the most of your days.[2]

Melville's Captain Ahab was a sailor and a hunter, but far more, he was a man in pursuit of an obsession: the great white whale. We all are pursuing something, and the object of our pursuit is what controls most of our energies and consumes most of our time.

While I once gave away too much time and money to things that are temporary, such as music and watching sports, I have settled in my mind what my *true* obsessions are: the welfare of my family and a bedrock commitment to God and my faith. Those are worth dying for. I don't want to die tangled in the ropes of some worthless pursuit, like Ahab drowning in the sea, lashed to the great white obsession that finally took him down. I want my life to have eternal consequences, so I build into the lives of my children the things they need for ultimate success.

Last week three of my friends met untimely deaths. One, a single dad with two teenagers, was killed in a car accident. Another (lost to a heart attack) had a three-year-old daughter. The third friend (lost to cancer) was married with three children. Only one of these men was older than forty-five. If their obsession was family, they at least left a legacy worth their efforts. Their families will continue the legacy of commitment to the foundational relationships: first to God, then to family, then a commitment to serve others.[3] The things these men did for their loved ones will endure. Single parenting is tough no matter how you go about it, so make it matter! Make sure your hard work endures for future generations.

Time is used best when you understand the concept of time within time. Time within time refers to real time lived inside the allotted twenty-four hours per day. It involves living in the moment and learning to build fun into every aspect of life.

Some people think I fail to grasp the gravity of the situation; others are convinced that I'm insane. Perhaps both theories are partially true, but that's not the real method behind my madness. The real reason was discovered by a friend back in 1978. I was working as a counselor at Camp Mountain Lake in Tracy City, Tennessee. That's when Rick Rogers revealed my secret. Some of the guys were offering theories to explain my erratic behavior. Was it for shock value or to attract attention? "No," Rick said. "You guys have it all wrong. Klumpp's not doing any of that. He's just entertaining himself."

Rick was right. I was always playing.

I've never lost my love for playing. In fact, the only truly miserable time in my life was when I began to take myself too seriously and ceased to play. I was making myself miserable, along with everyone who was depending on me. So here's the first rule of making the most of the moment: Don't take yourself too seriously. Second rule: Learn to play at whatever you do. If there is no time for play and no way to make what you're doing into a game, reassess its place in your life. If your job or mission in life is so important that there is no room for enjoyment, then look for something else to do.

Ironically, I have found this too-serious mode of living to be especially common among devoutly religious individuals. These folks have jobs just like everyone else. And they raise their kids and run errands and do household chores, and then they're also busy with ministry activities. Nothing wrong with that. I've been a pastor and a prison chaplain, and I'm as involved in my church as the next guy. But it's possible to be so busy that we lose sight of love and laughter and treasuring the precious children God has given us. Be careful that you don't squeeze the fun out of life.

Jesus himself was well aware of the danger of getting too busy doing good things. A woman named Martha, who was one of Jesus' closest friends, was your basic Type A personality. Jesus visited her home, and Martha threw herself into a frenzy of activity. Sadly, she was so preoccupied with whipping up a great meal that she missed the simple joy of sitting down for a conversation with Jesus. She was showing hospitality while denying herself the fun of entertaining her guest. Martha was a perfect example of a hard-working and well-meaning person who had squeezed the fun out of life.[4]

Learning to live in the moment and play at living is not easy. Because our culture rewards "important" contributions to business or society, we often seek recognition in those areas. This is sad, because our kids seem to land outside the categories of *serious* and *important,* and so they get lost in the process.

Let's stop and take a new look at the situation. Bottom line: God is in charge, and he emphasizes relationships. Nothing we do outside of human relationships will ultimately matter or last into eternity. Those who love you and need you most are living in your home. Your role as a single dad is as important as any role that exists in life. Do it well.

As for your self-image, it has taken a beating. Entering into marriage with the love of your life and dreaming of your future, raising a family together, building memories, enjoying each other for a lifetime—all of those dreams have died. And part of your confidence and self-image died with it. But now, as you rebuild your life, establish your self-image on a lasting foundation. Your relationship with God matters. Your children matter. You are loved by a God who will *never* forget about you even when you feel he is far away. Build upon these bedrock truths and be proud of the things you accomplish with your family. And while you're at it, enjoy your children every chance you get.

Each time you accomplish something of *real, eternal* worth, no matter how small it may seem, make note of it. You might want to record these successes in a separate notebook and review them from time to time. This reminds you that you're making real progress. Use journaling, matchbook covers, or other knickknacks as reminders of places and events and achievements that came about due to your commitment to God and your children. Make it personal and fun. You need these mile markers to help you measure your progress in keeping your focus on what really matters.

I had a friend who marked significant accomplishments—"Stayed home with the kids and played Risk instead of going to play pool"—on three-by-five-inch cards that he reviewed from time to time. It kept in focus the things he wanted to invest himself in. Over time, sacrificing for his family became more rewarding than he could have imagined, while the things he had previously enjoyed lost their attraction.

In coping, it is also important to reward yourself. In order to remain positive and keep burnout at arm's length, frequently treat yourself to something. Leave the house for a quiet walk. Get an iced coffee from the local coffee shop. Buy a hobby magazine. Whatever you enjoy, whatever you can afford, learn to reward yourself.

DO WONDERS
WITH LIMITED FINANCES

For those who know me well, hearing that I've included financial advice in a book for single dads will reduce them to laughter, or tears. Some of my friends would say that I've squandered fortunes and too many opportunities to keep track of. To others, I am some type of anomaly who never seems to have a career but always has enough to live well. Somehow I have managed to do most of the things that I want to do. That fact and the love of my children are how I measure success. Money is for living, not the opposite.

Having said that, I wouldn't be living under a roof and feeding and clothing my kids if it weren't for the hard work and kindness of friends and family members who came alongside with well-timed and much-needed help. Sometimes the "grace" of giving came through my supporters and contributors when I was in full-time ministry. Sometimes it came through my family. Sometimes it was a total mystery. It just appeared, with no one taking credit. Gifts such as these are outside our control. Remember, God is in charge; we're not.

One of my martial-arts instructors used to say, "You can be happy or you can be sad. It's your choice." I used to think he was grossly over-simplifying things. Then in my divorce I was thrust into a world that was totally out of my control. About the only thing I could control was how I would respond to my new circumstances. I remembered the wisdom of my karate instructor. He was a fifteen-year champion among experts in Japanese full-contact karate. He had been through a lot, and he knew that no matter what happens, life will go on. You can choose how you will approach any circumstance.

Eliminating Debt

When I began my journey as a single parent, I had been used to a fairly significant income. But I had accumulated a fair amount of recent debt by throwing money at my marital problems. I had no investment portfolio. I had a small amount of stock and property that had come my way through the generosity of my parents.

Before my divorce, but just as my wife and I were experiencing the highest degree of emotional separation, the company I'd been working for was sold and the management team was broken up. I needed work, and opportunities in that town were limited. So I began looking to relocate my family. Then my wife left, and I realized I needed to provide some stability for my kids. To keep from disrupting my children's lives even more, I stayed put and was forced to accept a different job at an 80 percent reduction in income.

My debt at that point included my home, two automobiles, and some credit-card bills. I was in the hole to the tune of $200,000. With a new, lower-paying job, I was bringing home $1,600 a month in income, but I faced a $750 monthly house payment, two auto loans at roughly $600 per month combined, and significant credit-card payments. And all that was on top of regular living expenses. To stay afloat financially, I began working three jobs and started selling off a good number of assets to reduce debt.

It was grim, but within three years I was able to return to financial solvency without filing bankruptcy. How I managed this is perhaps the subject for another book. Here are the basics:

- I cashed in stocks and retirement funds.
- I sold my automobiles and bought an older one. It wasn't flashy, but it got me to work and back.

- I negotiated payoff schedules with all of my creditors.
- I reduced my family's monthly budget to bare-bones status. We dropped cable, cell phone service, and even the kids' allowances.
- Eventually, I sold my home at a sacrifice.

None of this was easy, but I was guided by the principle that having no debt was my greatest asset. It's not a popular principle in our day, but it kept my kids fed and clothed and educated. And it kept me out of bankruptcy. I'm no financial wizard. When I have money I usually give it away or spend it. But having the responsibility of raising my kids well gave me a purpose and a bottom-line commitment to get my financial house in order.

Do yourself a favor by getting out of debt. Stop using credit and start paying off your debts. Cut your budget to the quick. Live within your means, even if you feel you can't. This hurts the most while getting started. However, it will be worth the struggle. Debt enslaves us. If, however, we get debt free, then we—rather than our creditors—determine what we'll do with our money. Give it to the church or to charity, save some, spend some on needed items or a vacation or to replace that old beater sitting in the driveway. There is tremendous freedom in eliminating debt.

Groceries on a Shoestring

Paying off debt is a long-range strategy, but what about the *daily* struggle of money management? Retailers want us to hand our money over to them, while we'd prefer to keep it in our wallets. But there's a way to work the system. By using the system to my advantage, I have managed to feed my four active, hungry troops on as little as $200 a month in the grocery budget. And I feed them well.

My daughter Paige, with the help of a family friend, learned the art of coupon shopping. We have stocked our cabinets with as much as $100 worth of sundry items for as little as $2. It takes skill, dedication, and a full mastery of coupon shopping. I would love to explain how Paige works this magic, but I can't. So I'll let Paige explain at the end of this chapter.

In the meantime, let me give you some tips for feeding the troops on a tight budget. The main issue is to learn to make a meal from what is available rather than having to shop for a specific number of items. The list of inexpensive kitchen staples from chapter 6—those things I said that I buy on autopilot—will give you the basic foodstuffs, which can easily be combined with items that are regularly on sale. If you live in an area with two or three major grocers, you need to know which items each store has on sale and which they regularly carry at reduced price. And refuse to be lured into impulse buys. Buy only what is on your list. If you come in for apples, don't grab bananas. Wait a few days, and the bananas will drop to thirty-nine cents or lower as they ripen. Know what a "good deal" actually is.

Sales tend to follow seasonal demands. You can get a mess of hot dogs around Labor Day and the Fourth of July for as little as sixty-nine cents a pack. So buy a bunch and freeze them. Buy store-brand bread or use the day-old shops for bread. You can reduce your price per loaf from ninety-nine cents and higher to sixty-nine cents and lower. These day-old shops are also great for finding cheap snack stuff for school lunches.

When you're fighting a schedule and a budget that are equally tight, convenience items like bagged salad look like salvation. Fight the urge. Keep those luxuries for times when you absolutely need them. A head of lettuce, two tomatoes, a cucumber, and a bag of carrots go a long way and make a ton of salad. Ultimately, waste management is also easier when you're working with the raw materials rather than a bag of ready-made salad, since the ready-made stuff will often wilt before you can eat all of it.

Having said that, you will need a few fallback items for the days when life spins out of control and you're pushed to the limit. Potpies are a personal favorite. When I'm too worn out to whip up a meal, it's suddenly potpie night. They can be purchased on sale for anywhere from three for a dollar to fifty cents each. Potpies and cheap frozen pizzas are gifts to this single parent from the hands of modern food science.

Cheap Entertainment

In the exhaustion of single parenting, one rationalization that invites over-spending goes something like this: You decide to take the kids to the movies. Tickets cost $7.50 for you and $5.50 for each child under twelve. You spend another $5 on popcorn. But everybody knows you can't have popcorn without cold beverages at $2.75 each. If you and two children split the popcorn, you just dropped more than $30 for two hours of relief.

"Well," the line of reasoning usually begins, "the kids and I have earned it. If nothing else, all the hurt and hardship we're going through has earned this and more." And these are most likely inarguable facts. You *have* suffered and you *do* need outlets for entertainment and relaxation. But you may not be able to afford them right now. We need to exercise restraint in our spending and trust that the reward promised by self-control will be sufficient.

As you practice restraint, though, don't kiss fun good-bye. Put some form of miscellaneous spending or entertainment allowance in your budget. Then manage your rewards carefully and effectively. You can treat yourself inexpensively. Rent an old movie, buy a box of microwave popcorn, get a two-liter bottle of root beer, and turn off the phone. Now your total cash outlay is closer to $6. For another $10 you can go wild and eat out at Taco Bell. You're still at half the cost of going to a movie at a theater. And when all is said and done, it's the love and comfort of doing something as a family that will make the evening a treasure.

Now let me put things in perspective. When times are tough, we want everything in these precious moments with our kids to be perfect. Don't cause yourself this torture. Inevitably, you're opening yourself for frustration. Just as you all settle down with popcorn for a long-awaited video, someone will stop by. The phone will ring because you forgot to turn it off. The popcorn will burn. Someone will spill root beer on the carpet. These simple frustrations can become volcanic interruptions in the land of unrealistic expectations. Don't let it get to you. Emotions are already strained in the single-dad family. So keep your expectations realistic.

Tell the folks at the door that it's bad timing—they caught you at a family time. Let the phone ring, and when it stops, turn off the ringer. Whoever is calling will get over it. If one of the kids spills his soda pop, wipe it up. Remember, you can be happy or you can be sad. It's your choice.

Reap the Rewards of Managed Anger

"Have Anger. Will Parent" could be the motto on the business card of most of the single dads I know. Anger seems to be a standard part of the equation whether we like it or not. While there is often initial anger during and after divorce, what I am more concerned with is the anger that rises and falls as part of the mourning process. It's a type of self-pity: "Why did this happen to me?" Or it's impatience: "When am I going to get a break?"

Anger is a secondary emotion, an outward expression of our inward hurt. This hurt is often from the grieving process over our now-dead dreams. With the anger comes blame. "How could I have been so stupid?" or "Why did I let her do this to me?"

Let's back out of this cycle. First, remember that blame is useless. It doesn't matter who's at fault—and actually you're *both* at fault to some degree. Face the issues as they are. You're a single dad, and your kids have real needs. Your ex did whatever she did, and it's done. You messed up too, and that's also done and in the past. Reverse the negative emotion and deal with the raw facts. Allow yourself the opportunity to hurt. Cry if the time is right. Take a deep breath and refocus if crying is not appropriate. Acknowledge the hurt and get back in the game.

In one style of martial arts, we used to shout the word *osu!* It's a Japanese word formed by the pictograph of one hand pushing another person upward. *Osu!* has multiple applications from "Yes sir" to "Hello." The root idea is "respect," beginning with self-respect. I often say the word quietly or silently in my mind. It is my refocus-and-move-on word. I use it to interrupt a negative thought pattern, to hold back the emotional tide, regroup, and get back to the task at hand. Use a meaningful word or phrase, a prayer, or a verse of Scripture to move you from a negative track onto a constructive path.

As a karate instructor I work with many families who are looking for solutions to anger. So based on my own life and those I've worked with closely, here are a few strategies for anger management that might help you and your family:

- *Step back.* Stop and identify the real source of your anger. Then count to ten before you say anything.
- *Take a walk.* Getting away from the situation and giving yourself a moment to think and calm down can work wonders. Plus a brisk walk helps work off some tension.
- *Exercise.* A regular regimen of exercise will help reduce the stress level in your life. You don't have to wait until you're angry. But if you're really mad about something, that's a good time to jog, ride a bicycle or an exercise bike, punch the heavy bag, or do fifty push-ups. Send the energy somewhere else until you're in touch with your hurt.
- *Cry.* No kidding! Most anger grows out of pain and frustration. If you can get in touch with the pain and channel your emotions through another God-given release mechanism, you might be surprised at the relief you experience. Once you decide that crying isn't just for babies, you may also find that a few tears start coming more naturally and more frequently, and they're doing you a world of good.
- *Take a swing.* My friend keeps two foam bats at home. Whenever the kids get under each other's skin, out come the bats and they pound away on something that can't be damaged by a foam bat. And while they take their swings, they holler out their frustrations.
- *Journal.* Write down your feelings. Write a letter telling your journal *exactly* what you think and feel. The wonder of a journal

is that you can say whatever you want. There is no one to tell you that you shouldn't feel that way or that you need to get your act together.

- *Get it off your chest.* Turn an empty chair so that it is facing you. Imagine the source of your anger sitting there and then let lose. Shout, scream, cry, or just talk in a normal tone of voice. The point is to tell the "listener" everything you feel needs to be said at the moment. Sometimes talking out loud can help you sort out your thoughts and feelings. (It's best to do this when the kids aren't home. They might begin to wonder about your mental stability if they notice you shouting at an empty chair.)

As I have taught karate over the years, I've noticed that most anger problems seem to dissipate as my students grow in confidence and self-esteem. It's not the kicking and punching of karate that make the difference, but the self-respect they derive from pushing themselves, achieving, and being part of a team. When we struggle with difficulty and overcome it, we benefit from the affirmation that "I really can do this. I won't let this defeat me!"

If you find that your anger is not mitigated by the basic strategies mentioned earlier, you may want to consider counseling. A counselor can help identify your problem and will provide additional strategies for getting your emotions under control. Following are behaviors that signal a significant anger problem:

- Do you explode over some minor incident, erupting and lashing out at whoever is present?

- Do you often feel shame or remorse after an explosion, knowing that you were lashing out at someone who had nothing to do with the real problem?

- Do you lash out in anger without knowing why?
- Do you throw things or strike inanimate objects (the wall, a piece of furniture, your car) when angry?
- Do you make threats to control or intimidate others?
- Do you become a bully, picking on someone weaker than yourself?
- Do you grab or strike others when angry?

If you answered yes to any of these questions, don't be afraid to get help. Getting to the source of your anger and getting well will bring a great sense of relief and freedom. For additional ideas, check out online resources such as www.angermgmt.com.

The Path to Success

Time, finances, anger. These are make-or-break issues for a single dad. It's much easier to find the success strategies when we think clearly about the realities we face as single parents.

Here are the facts: The work of raising kids is never done, and now you're doing it alone. You're covering two bases, and you're severely short-handed. You can choose to feel victimized, since you've been left to do all the work. Or you can choose to be thankful that you've been entrusted with a precious mission. You have the privilege of leading your children through their growing-up years.

I view it as a privilege that I am trusted with the lives of my children. When cabin fever sets in and I'd rather be out with the guys, I remind myself that the lives of my children are of utmost importance. They will someday grow up, and that's when I'll pursue my hobbies and other diversions. For now, however, I have a higher priority—the welfare of my kids.

Planning occasional times out with friends is not a bad thing. Neither is it bad to have friends over. Just be certain that the frequency of time spent with friends is in balance with your family time and that all of your priorities with family are in order first. When I was getting my bearings as a single dad, I had friends over about every six weeks. This provided some relief from tension and cabin fever, and it also kept me nearby so my kids could reach me if they needed me. There were added benefits when my kids stayed home during guys' night. Not only did my children's presence keep us adults responsible, but it gave the kids a feeling that they were a fun part of my life and cool enough to hang out with Dad and his buddies.

There's plenty you can do with friends without having to leave the house. Have a Super Bowl party. Host a bring-your-own-meat barbecue night and grill what your buddies bring over. If some of the guys hunt, you might get some odd and tasty things to grill. Have a movie night or a card tournament.

On nights when I went out with friends, I made certain the children could find me and always gave them a timetable for my return. As long as I kept these outings to once or twice a month, all seemed to go well.

Find proactive solutions to the issues rather than stewing in your anger or being consumed by self-pity. Find some appropriate support for your single-dad lifestyle. But be careful. A group of angry or bitter friends will do nothing to advance your cause. Find friends who will come in and assist you when burnout is near. Find friends who will cook with you, clean with you, listen to you. At times, ask a friend to watch your kids for a few hours while you get out of the house. If you don't occasionally get off by yourself or with a few close friends, you'll really go mad. So occasionally catch a movie or grab a cup of coffee with friends. If your children are well cared for, they won't feel cheated.

The strategies for daily success outlined in this chapter will make a world of difference. Once you get a handle on making the most of your time, getting by on limited finances, and reaping the rewards of managed anger, your life will take a turn for the better. You'll begin to enjoy the tremendous freedom that comes with being on top of things, rather than always being buried underneath it all.

Survival Tips

$145 Worth of Groceries for 42 Cents

When I first heard of people buying bundles of groceries with next to no money, I was skeptical. In fact, if my daughter had not been trained in coupon shopping by a family friend, and had I not seen the evidence, I still wouldn't believe it's possible to get groceries for such a minimal cash expenditure. Do keep in mind that timing is everything. Grocers often change their coupon policies, depending on local competition among stores and the seasonal demand for and availability of certain products. The greater the competition and the stronger the local market, the more likely stores will be to double and even triple the value of coupons. Newspapers, especially Sunday and Wednesday editions, are crammed with coupons. But also keep your eye on periodicals that cater to women, since these publications frequently feature higher-discount coupons on certain products.

But enough from me. I'll let you hear the story from a real pro. One morning I took Paige to a local coffee shop, and while she sipped hot chocolate and I drank a cup of coffee, I asked her to tell the tale of coupon shopping.

"Well," she said, "the first step was to learn to cut coupons and organize them. You buy some Sunday newspapers and look for coupons for up to seventy-five cents. It could be anything. I was taught just to clip and sort everything I found."

Paige's coupon-shopping teacher, Barbie Hames, knew a store that tripled the value of all coupons, and she sorted the coupons according to how items are stocked, aisle by aisle, in that store. She

(continued)

placed the sorted coupons in a file envelope. On triple-coupon day, Paige and Barbie would go early and buy the items they had coupons for. Paige notes, "I was able to buy some neat stuff, like shaving cream for my legs, that I wouldn't get if I was paying for it."

This is how Paige and Barbie made a killing on grocery shopping. If a coupon was worth seventy-five cents off deodorant, the tripled coupon was worth $2.25, but the deodorant might only cost $1.49. "They won't give you the extra money in change," Paige clarified, "but you can use the credit against other items. So if I bought ten of that deodorant, I got ten free and made $7.60 in additional credits. I could buy $7.60 of groceries for nothing. And if you were using coupons for the other purchases, the $7.60 really went a long way. There are some great coupons for anything from salad dressing to macaroni dishes and spaghetti sauce.

"Then we sometimes used coupons from passbooks that gave $5 off any purchase of $50 or more. If you use that one first, you save the $5 before using your other coupons." (Schools often sell such passbooks—books full of coupons for local retailers—as fund-raisers. For an example of such a book, see www.entertainment.com.)

Paige got better at this with practice. "The first time I bought $80 in groceries for $16," she reported. "When I got the hang of it, I was able to go through the line a couple of times and really stock up. I once bought almost $200 worth of groceries for about $8 and got a free turkey! My all-time best was $145 of groceries for forty-two cents."

My hat is off to my daughter. I asked Paige to summarize, for the benefit of us dads. Here's the deal:

- Find a supermarket that triples the value of coupons. (You may not be able to find a triple-coupon store in your area. If so, double coupons will still save you money and the system will work to a degree.)

- Keep your eye out for coupons in the newspaper and in magazines, especially those worth fifty cents or more for relatively low-cost items.

- Buy coupon items as much as possible and save other shopping for another time.

- Practice! Practice! Practice!

A side note: My friend Barbie Hames, Paige's "coupon mentor," is known to keep a whole room of her house stocked with items from coupon sales. Sometimes cashiers, store managers, and customers would get aggravated with the wait in line or the seeming greed of it all. Who needs twenty-five jars of picante sauce or thirty boxes of cereal? But those items paid for others. Besides, Barbie has not only taught her methods to single moms and families of limited financial means, she stocks up on items and then invites those less fortunate than herself to come and select a trunk full of free groceries. Many times she helped my family eat well, smell better, and generally feel good about ourselves. Everyone needs a friend like Barbie. Way to go, girl! Also, many thanks to the stores that promote double- and triple-coupon sales.

8

THE SMART BET
FOR SINGLE DADS

One Investment That's Guaranteed to Pay Off

WE SINGLE DADS need something we can rely on to carry us through the stressful days and sleepless nights of single parenting. My first suggestion is to concentrate on the things that last—our kids and their future.

In doing research for this book, I spoke to many brokenhearted and burned-out men. But whenever we started talking about their children, *wham!* They were all smiles. When I interviewed Rick, for instance, he was having financial difficulties and was in the midst of an unexpected career change. He was deeply troubled about his future. But when we talked about his relationship with his children, the stress seemed to melt away.

"I love my children with all my heart and soul," he said. "I would do anything for them. I'm not afraid to express myself with them. They're the best friends I have and will ever have."

John, another single dad, is often lonely and misses the pulse of his relationship with his ex-wife. But to watch his eyes light up, you only have to ask about his daughter. Though John is a success in his field and has been a leader in every initiative he has undertaken, it's his children who bring him the most joy.

I've asked John about his days as an NCAA Division I quarterback. He has a Southwest Conference Championship ring on his finger—commemorating one of the few conference championships Baylor University can claim. The details of his stories about college sports are generally vague, and while he takes some delight in answering my football questions, he is only marginally enthusiastic. Ask about his kids, though, and he'll go on in vivid detail about the events in their lives, hardly pausing to take a breath.

There is no question that our children are a tremendous blessing. Yet with the pressures of single parenting, it's possible to lose or at least misplace this truth. To put it in perspective for a young artist friend, I said, "You may be an incredible performer and songwriter. Yet the chance of your writing the one piece of music or poetry that lasts beyond this generation and continues to make an impact hundreds of years from now is probably a trillion to one. But the chance that one of your descendants will still be making an impact on the world hundreds of years from now is almost a sure thing."

What matters for future generations is the people you invest in, not the accomplishments you can claim. Your relationships are the only thing of lasting worth, and your children represent your most precious relationships.

Find Your Joy

Finding joy in the heritage you will leave behind is part of the spiritual order of our world. But keeping our focus on that joy amid all the pressures and problems is sometimes almost impossible. How do we stay joyful when our kids don't follow our guidance, misuse the things we give them, and squander every good opportunity we provide?

The answers to these tough questions lie in spiritual reality. God exists, and he loves us. Scripture tells us that God actually takes delight in us.[1] So the question of how we can maintain a focus on the blessings that our children are is to see them as God sees us—as his own children. God's unconditional love, grace, and mercy—and his timely and motivating swat on our rear when necessary—all contribute to our growth. And his model of perfection in parenting us enhances our ability to parent our children well and to regard them with true joy.

Consider the parenting model that God provides for us. The Bible tells us that a loving father disciplines his children.[2] Grace and mercy that are not balanced with boundaries and reprimands are license, not love. Loving our children involves preparing them for life—all of life, not just the good and easy parts. In real life, our choices, decisions, and actions bring consequences. Disciplining our children teaches them that their actions have very real consequences. Neglect discipline and you will reap children who will be spoiled, demanding, out of control, and unhappy.

The key to success in this area is investing heavily in their early years. If 80 percent of a child's personality is formed between three and six years of age, then the need for building into their life and establishing healthy doses of love and discipline is greatest during this time.[3] I would caution against letting your children run amuck when they are toddlers with the excuse, "They'll have lots of time later on to learn about rules and discipline. So let 'em have fun while they can."

Let your kids explore their world and experience the wonder of childhood. Wrap them in your love and let them have plenty of fun. But don't let them operate without restraints. The result of boundary-free parenting is often tragic in the lives of children.

Psalm 127 tells us that God is the source of prosperity, and interestingly, prosperity is not described as material wealth. Prosperity is instead equated with having children. Then the plot thickens. We are reminded that the big payoff from this investment comes one day in the future, when our children will contend for *us* at the gate.[4] That means that when we are old, we'll have children who love us and are committed to assuring our well-being when we're not able to care for ourselves. No matter how self-sufficient you once were, it is a joy to know there is someone looking out for you as your strength declines. I want strong sons and daughters to argue my case and defend my life when I am no longer able to do these things for myself.

As a martial artist I've learned the rude truth that we can't always continue to perform as we once did. I am not the warrior I once was, and in twenty years I won't be the warrior I am today. But amid these personal losses of agility and quickness, I know that everything I invest in my children will be there for me when I need someone to come to my aid. And I'm not ashamed to admit that someday I will let them take care of me.

But it's not just the future rewards I'm looking forward to. It's the immediate riches as well. As I invest in the lives of my children, they return the love in our present family life. Not long ago my daughter, who is working for a law firm, took some of her money and bought me a giant barbecue smoker for Father's Day. There is little that I enjoy more than sitting in my backyard and cooking enough meat for a football team. The love is flowing here. Likewise with my youngest. If I'm having a tough day and Nico gets wind of it, without my ever saying a word there are two small but strong hands rubbing my shoulders to take away the tension. This is the prosperity I desire.

Go for Quality in Every Moment

When a dad is busy from 5:30 A.M. until 6:00 P.M., just keeping his job and supporting his family, moments become a lot more precious. I still hear parents talk about the importance of spending "quality" time with children. Which makes me wonder, *Is there such a thing as nonquality time?*

I love life. I want *every* moment to be quality. If I am sorting doorknobs on an assembly line, I want it to be enjoyable and memorable. What adds quality to a moment is the attitude you bring. Of course, fishing with my son is supposed to be more enjoyable than doing laundry with him, but does the latter have to be drudgery? Paul, one of the greatest teachers of the first century, talked about having learned the secret to being content in any circumstance. For him, it didn't matter if he was destitute or financially comfortable. It didn't even matter if he was free to walk the streets or chained to a guard in a Roman prison.[5] A life filled with joy and acceptance of the moment doesn't bother to distinguish between want and plenty. Contentment begins with your attitude.

Whether I'm fishing with my kids or doing laundry with them, I care deeply about being with them, and I work to maintain an attitude that is gracious and thankful and positive. If I'm happy, they're happy.

If we are communicating and sharing, whether playing games or preparing dinner, we're enjoying quality time.

Remember the advice of one of my martial-arts instructors: "You can be happy or you can be sad. The choice is yours." So why not choose to be happy? Choose to turn your life and even the challenging task of single parenting into moments of fun.

Fun comes in many forms, and we cheat ourselves if we limit it to prescribed times of being entertained and amused. If you are tired, broke, and pushed for time, you'll find that life quickly deteriorates to drudgery due to the sheer grind of living—especially if you limit your fun to outside distractions and prepackaged forms of amusement. If you impose such limits, you'll be miserable, stressed out, short on time and money, and clueless about what to do about it.

That was me after my divorce. I was dying for some escape in the form of entertainment, but too pressed for time and money to go to the movies, go out to dinner, go to a concert, or run out of town for a breather. Then I realized that I didn't need packaged diversions to be entertained. So I decided to "deculturize" myself. Today, I don't follow the story line of any television hospital drama or crime series, and I no longer read the entertainment section of the newspaper to see what's going on this weekend that might provide some momentary escape. Instead of scanning the paper for the next game worth watching, I have created my own game. My game is life.

LEARN TO SIT STILL

I have learned how to sit still, be at peace, and not get antsy or bored, worrying that I'm wasting my time or missing out on something. I have learned to enjoy the moment, no matter what the moment brings (or fails to bring).

For starters, there is a fabulous drama outside my window. Each day the scenery gives way to change, often from rain to fog and on to sunshine. The cats on my porch play at their own form of martial-arts sparring. I love watching the birds or just seeing the clouds float across the sky. At first these displays seemed to move way too slow. They just didn't provide enough action and excitement to be entertaining. But I continued practicing one thing: sitting still. And with practice, I turned ordinary, easily overlooked natural phenomena from a boring backdrop to a vivid, exciting daily parade.

A few thousand years ago, God gave us this directive: "Be still, and know that I am God."[6] God wants us to know the value of stillness, quiet, and stepping out of the rat race from time to time. In quietness, we often encounter God in a way unlike any other setting. But being still, for most of us, is a near impossibility. So how do we learn to just sit there quietly, doing absolutely nothing?

I asked this question for years. I would sit quietly while ten thousand things raced through my head. It wouldn't be long before I'd jump up, thinking, *This is no good. I've got too many things to do!* Then I'd rush off to do something.

Well, hold on to your shorts. I've got news for you. There is nothing "to do." Yep! I didn't stutter. There's nothing to do. All you Type A's can now stop pounding your fists at the absurdity of my statement. Bear with me for a moment (you can spare that much time).

Remember what matters and what lasts: the people you invest your life in. One hundred years from now, few, if any, of our accomplishments will matter. Our big achievements won't even be a blip on the radar screen. Most of the really important things have to do with *who we are* rather than *what we accomplish.* Our skills and talents and hard work just aren't that significant in the grand scheme of things.

Don't panic. That doesn't mean we should quit our jobs and go sit silently on a mountaintop, being still for God. We still have to exert effort, of course. But what this truth means is that we can be free from striving.

"Be still, and know that I am God." Another translation of that verse reads, "Cease striving and know that I am God."[7]

For most of us single dads, *striving* could be our middle name. We're striving to overcome the hurt and rejection of divorce. We're striving to keep everything moving ahead and all the bases covered and all of our kids in one piece—and doing these things with one hand tied behind our backs. We go to work and strive to meet sales quotas and deadlines and to beat the time clock. Striving is something we know well, something we have mastered. The idea of sitting still might as well be a foreign language.

It's difficult, to be sure, but not impossible. Sitting still, like any new skill, begins with practice. It takes discipline. It involves an attitude of accepting things as they are, not fueling our anger by wishing things were somehow better. Being satisfied and finding joy are two things that refuse to coexist with striving.

Sitting still begins when you can stop comparing. Your life is your life, better than some, worse than others. But where you stand relative to others doesn't matter. Comparison breeds envy, which breeds contempt. And pretty soon, you'll feel contempt toward yourself because you don't measure up to someone else. So let go of it. You are created in God's image.[8] God loves you, so learn to love yourself. Once you do this, instead of comparing your lot in life with others', you may be surprised at how much beauty and wonder you will begin to see in the world around you.

As the striving falls away, stillness can take its place. You can again look at colors and marvel at their brilliance or feel the breeze and be thankful for the sensation. You can find pleasure in a moment of stillness. Only then can you stop your frantic striving toward the next big thing that will finally bring pleasure and contentment. The truth is, it won't deliver what you're looking for. So stop striving.

Take the Striving Test

Here's a quick quiz to help you gauge your ability to stop striving. You leave work later than you intended, hop in your car, and then realize you need to stop at the grocery store on the way home. It won't take that long to pick up milk and bread and a few ingredients for tonight's dinner. So you detour on your way home to get these few groceries. As you're driving, you remember that you promised your kids you'd be home by 6:00, but you don't get to the store until 5:45. You hurry through the aisles collecting your groceries, and then whip your cart into the shortest checkout line. There are two shoppers in line ahead of you.

This is where the cease-striving test really beings.

The elderly customer at the head of the line has decided to write a check…slowly. Plus she enjoys visiting with the store clerk. All forward momentum in the checkout line has ground to a halt.

What do you do, other than steal a quick glimpse at your watch? Are your insides churning? Are you tapping your fingers on the handle of the shopping cart? Do you glare at the check-writing customer? Do you simmer and smolder and silently berate the heavens because you, especially on this day, had to stop at the market and get in line behind the number one, world champion, clueless shopper? Or do you relax and practice your patience, knowing that impatient behavior won't get you through the line any sooner?

Let's say you passed this first test. Congratulations! You were able to be still and savor life even while that first customer, after receiving a receipt for her purchase, remembered that she needed a pack of gum and then began carefully counting out eighty-seven pennies from her purse to pay for it. You're taking a deep breath and you're doing great.

But…now the next customer in line—the customer just ahead of you—is stepping up to the cash register. He has twelve items, and he's in the ten-item-or-fewer line. Plus three of his items require a price check. "Bakery, call line 6, please. Bakery…line 6. Dairy, call line 6. Dairy…"

How are you doing? Any quickening of the pulse and clenching of the jaw—or fists? Stomach tightening yet? Hey, I feel your pain. Or at least, I used to feel it. Now, whenever I wait in line at the grocery or anywhere else, I enjoy the freedom of stillness. I use that moment to refresh. I breathe easy. I relax. I study something that is pleasing to my eye—the potted plants for sale near the checkout lines or the giggling toddler with his mom in the next line. I smile at the toddler. I don't force that smile, either. It comes naturally.

But I've had to *practice* being still. I have forced myself to practice listening, relaxing, focusing on the moment. I've had to tell myself over and over the true things that I need to be reminded of, rather than listening to voices within that cause me to strive after nothing. It doesn't matter if I'm fifteen minutes late getting home. Having the privilege of going home to my kids after work is a reward and a blessing. Fifteen minutes this way or that makes absolutely no difference.

God has opened my eyes to a new reality that has brought peace to my days. He says that I am wonderfully made. I am bought with a price. God will never leave me. My children are my gift from God. All ambition is striving after wind. Loving myself is the beginning of loving others. God loves me. God loves you, too.[9]

I've started putting up index cards around my house and office to remind me of how good I really have it. I even put up phrases that remind me of goals I'm aiming for: "I am thin." "I am at peace." These are tangible reminders that help me keep a positive focus and attitude. A positive outlook goes hand in hand with a thankful and joyful spirit. Why be sad when you can be joyful? Choose the latter.

WHAT ABOUT WORK?

After all this talk about not striving, we still have chores at home and errands to run and kids to raise. And that doesn't even begin to get at the biggest time burner: Work! But why *do* we go to work? The obvious answer is to pay the rent and buy groceries and pay doctor's bills and college tuition and buy new shoes for the kids and orthodontia and… But those are the external reasons. There is a much more important reason that we go to work every day.

Many dads work to acquire money, status, prestige, and other marks of career success. Working, for them, is a means of getting ahead in life, getting noticed, getting their ego stroked. I'm familiar with this drive to achieve. I grew up in a family with those same goals. However, I never bought into it. During a recent visit with my brother after the death of our mom, we were waxing philosophic when he threw me what I consider a wonderful compliment: "Your life has not been without its financial ups and downs that the rest of the family criticizes, but you've managed well enough. You've thoroughly lived life, doing things that mattered and that you enjoyed while meeting your responsibilities. You never compromised to chase a buck."

He was describing my commitment to quality over quantity and lasting meaning over short-term pleasure. It's not an issue of moral rightness or wrongness so much as it's a matter of personal values and living them out.

When I became a single dad, these values were put to the test. Until then, I'd been somewhat restless as I looked for the perfect setting in which I could live my life and pursue my passions—drama, writing, directing, and painting. Over the years, I have been a football coach, teacher, pastor, chaplain, plumber, bouncer, tankerman, deckhand, yacht salesman, car salesman, comic, actor, director, poet, playwright, riding instructor, camp director, centrifuge technician, lumberyard worker, cook, and karate instructor, just to name a few. I always viewed paid work as a necessary evil. Once I was a single dad, however, I was able to learn to enjoy whatever job I had, just for the job itself.

I needed the work to support my kids, but I also realized that work is a means to something else—fulfillment, a sense of being where God wants me, and a source of enjoyment and mission. As a single dad, I leave the house every morning because my job—with all its demands and aggravations, with all of its tedium and inconvenience—makes it possible for me not only to feed my children but also to support them in life. It gives me joy to earn a living that makes it possible for four kids named Klumpp to get established in their own lives.

If the opportunity to feed and clothe my family is a grace, then it is much harder for me to take my job for granted. If my job is this crucial to the success of my family as a whole, then preserving my employment through extra effort is not a chore but a joy. It's the "I was sad because I had no shoes until I met the man who had no legs" idea, but with a twist. Yes, being aware of those who have less gives us a better perspective on what we possess. But that's only one piece of the puzzle. Having anything at all, when we have no power to guarantee even one more breath, helps us realize that even a breath of air is a completely undeserved gift from God. We should be overwhelmed with gratitude that we can get out of bed in the morning and hug our kids and enjoy conversation and laughter.

The things that steal our joy are distortions of this truth. The distortion is that we "deserve" a better life or more money or less stress. If we believe we have a right to more ease, we're left feeling cheated because we're getting less than we feel we deserve. We are miserable, but it's because we bought into a lie. The solution is simple, really. Stop and be still. Give thanks for what you have. Declare out loud, "I have enough and I am happy and satisfied." Then live that way every day—while you're at work, with your kids, cooking meals, and doing chores. Whatever you're doing, take joy in it and consider it a gift from the hand of God.

Of course, some dads find their identity in their career. They love their job and brag to their friends about all they're accomplishing. For them the struggle is to find their identity in who they *are* instead of what they *do*. This is a cultural struggle as well. Ask a man about himself, and more often than not he'll say "I'm an attorney" or "I'm a division manager for such and such a company." That's what he does, and it's likely that he does it very well. But it's not even close to who the man is.

Our God-appointed identity was formed in our mother's womb and led forth by the plan of God. We are, at this time, dads. We are providers. We are priests of the family in prayer and counsel and spiritual leadership. We are protectors. We are the patriarchs of our own tribes. We have the privilege of reflecting the love of God as we love those around us.[10] And as we love and serve others, we *begin* with those closest to us—our kids.[11]

INVEST WHERE YOU'LL GET THE BIGGEST RETURN

I have a plaque that reads, "A truly wealthy man is one whose children will run into his arms even when his hands are empty." Before this adage can become true for you, you must decide to make it true. Do you value relationships more than possessions? And is it true for you that it would be enough to guard the relationships that you cherish even if all your money and possessions were suddenly taken from you?

Big-screen televisions, cars, and other stuff can be distractions that enhance the enjoyment of life but *only* if they enhance relationships. A camper or a boat can open up tremendous trips and fishing adventures with your kids. But a new truck and boat and camper in and of themselves will never make you happy. If you are an unhappy person and you purchase a big-screen television or a new stereo, you will simply become an unhappy person with lots of cool stuff. The things in your life will never make you happy.

Stuff isn't even a good investment of your money. It quickly loses value. The only guaranteed investment is that of your time, love, and training in a well-raised child. That effort will produce a guaranteed return of someone to call when you are old and lonely, someone to take you to lunch when you are no longer mobile, or someone to visit you when you are sick. The best and greatest human relationship of all, your children, is also the best and greatest investment of all.

You must be patient though. It takes a lifetime to prove the value of this investment. You may have a tendency to prejudge your efforts. Don't be shortsighted and don't lose hope. When your children disappoint you, remember that life is a learning experience. Children must make decisions, sometimes misguided ones, in order to learn to make a wise decision the next time. As they begin to make their own decisions, you are there to keep them from choosing anything that would bring lasting harm. The return on your relational investment will outlive you as your grandchildren and great-grandchildren reap the benefits of the time and effort you put into your own children.

When I asked my kids to recall some special times in our lives, their warm memories blew me away. It wasn't the trip to Germany or outings to Six Flags. It wasn't how much money I spent on them. It was the simple times.

Ian, my older son, cherishes a time when he and I went outside at midnight with a gas tiller we had borrowed. Midnight seemed like as good a time as any to chew up the side yard to make a garden. It was crazy, and for years we have laughed about all the racket we made and the insanity of gardening at midnight. It's a cherished memory for my son and me. And it cost nothing.

Interestingly, many of my children's most cherished memories are from the time after our family split. This is counterintuitive, I know. But it's also cause for encouragement. It took that tragic break to pull my family out of the cultural pattern of hurry, hurry, hurry. The need to bond and to put extra energy and attention into building and solidifying relationships became more urgent. We took advantage of the opportunity and made the most of it.

The investment your children want and need most is the investment of your life, your time, your attention, your training, and your love. Spend these things on your children and spend lavishly.

Survival Tips

A Dozen Ways to Invest Well

Here are twelve things you can do to make the best investment in your children—the one investment with a guaranteed return:

1. Love them unconditionally and tell them regularly that you love them no matter what happens.
2. Compliment their strengths regularly.
3. Compliment them in front of others.
4. Take an interest in their culture.
   - Reserve comments about their music and clothing for a later time, not while they are trying to show you their world.
   - Give them room to be themselves.
5. Ask questions that matter.
   - Ask specific questions about their lives that demonstrate your genuine interest.
   - Listen carefully to their answers.
6. Spend time with them doing something simple when the emphasis is on them and not the event.
7. Keep in mind their likes and dislikes.
8. Remember the significant dates in their lives.
9. Get to know their friends and take an interest in those friends.
10. Drop by and see them at school sometime.
11. Take pictures of them and share the pictures with friends and relatives who care about your kids.
12. Keep their pictures in your wallet, office, bedside, or other personal space.

┌─────────┐
│   9   │
└─────────┘

Hot Dogs: A Gift from God

Doable Meals That Won't
Give Your Kids Indigestion

"COOKING? SORRY, dads aren't well suited for the culinary arts, and especially for all the pots and pans and odd utensils that go with it."

Is that so? The way I see it, this is another fine opportunity for growth. I've read most of the Scriptures and many of the major philosophies of the Western world. There is no biblical or philosophical prohibition of men becoming proficient in the kitchen. As a matter of fact, the Bible tells us fairly early—in Genesis—that Jacob made a mean lentil stew.[1] And we later learn that Jesus grilled fish for breakfast.[2]

Preparing superior meals does not require a feminine touch. So wake up and smell the coffee or the lasagna or whatever it is your kids want you to fix for dinner. You want to eat? Get in the kitchen and figure it out.

On the other hand, it's not fair for anyone to be sent into the kitchen unarmed. There are a few simple habits and some basic recipe ideas that go a long way toward ensuring success at meal preparation. In addition, the *Joy of Cooking* cookbook is filled with simple tips for cooking and is a worthwhile purchase.

Cooking is pretty simple stuff, but there is more to it than heating water and tossing some macaroni into the pot. There are some basic rules to keep in mind. For example, egg noodles don't take as long to cook as spaghetti. If you overcook any type of pasta it turns to paste. And don't be fooled by the fire being turned off underneath the pot. If the water is still hot, the food still cooks. If you drained the pasta, run some cool water over it to stop the cooking process and limit sticking. Also, electric stoves continue to emit heat even after the element is turned off. Once the coil cools, the cooking stops, but that takes awhile. So if you're cooking on an electric stove, move the pot to another surface or another cool burner to stop the cooking process.

Cooking requires the right tools. Keep your utensils in a convenient place near the stove. You'll also need an assortment of pots and pans. (See the Survival Tips at the end of this chapter for a list of essential kitchen tools.) Cooking utensils should be like shop tools—get what you need. Your cooking habits are yours and yours alone. There are some rules of the road for family meals, but the real issue is whether it tastes good and serves the body's fuel needs.

Learn what flavors and spices your kids like. Use a short list of spices that work for you and experiment when you have the time and money to be wrong. Use taste as a guide. If it tastes funny to you it will probably taste funny to your kids. And remember, salt can always be added later. Don't overdo the salt when cooking.

I keep salt, seasoned salt, black pepper, garlic salt, garlic powder, onion powder, oregano, basil, thyme, celery salt, and dill on hand. With that mix I can do a lot of cooking. Add to it some barbecue sauce, Worcestershire sauce, soy sauce, olive oil, and lemon pepper or lemon juice and you can work subtle magic for most taste buds. You also need some sugar—or a sugar substitute. Throw in baking powder and baking soda and you can do just about anything, right down to baking biscuits from scratch.

Remember the KISS method: Keep It Simple Sir (we're remaining positive here). Boiling a hot dog is easier than whipping up cordon bleu. Fortunately, there are enough easy recipes to get you through life that provide good nutrition and plenty of variety while keeping cooking disasters from blowing up in your face.

Here is a generous helping of recipes and practical menus to get you through.

Menu Ideas

I'm not real cozy with the food pyramid and would never be confused with a nutritionist. These menu ideas are ones I've used regularly. They're easy to prepare, and my kids seem to enjoy eating them. Here's a sample menu for a week's worth of dinners.

Monday—Spaghetti and Meat Sauce, Garlic Bread, Tossed Salad

Boil water in a large pot. While the water is coming to a boil, brown the ground meat in a skillet over medium-high heat. Drain the meat after browning to reduce the fat content. There is no need to add spices, but a little salt is okay. If you like onions or garlic, they can be browned for a few minutes in a little margarine or oil first and then added to the meat.

Once your water is boiling, add spaghetti and cook until tender. (The package will have a recommendation as to how many minutes.) While the pasta is cooking, pour a container or two of spaghetti sauce into the meat and mix. You may want to season the sauce with oregano, basil, sugar, or a bit of wine or vinegar, depending on your taste. I like my sauce salty tart with lots of garlic, so in addition to garlic, I add salt, a little sugar, and vinegar. Lower your heat slightly and let your sauce simmer. When the spaghetti is tender, drain it and then run cool water over it to keep it from sticking. It'll become room temperature, but the sauce will warm it back up.

Turn your attention now to the bread and the salad. If you bought prepared garlic bread (there are tasty varieties from $1.69 to $3.00), just follow the directions on the bag. If you're striking out on your own in a wave of culinary independence, split a loaf of French bread (or lay out the sandwich slices). Melt butter in a small saucepan and add garlic from a garlic press. Or you can take soft margarine and stir in garlic powder. Choose whatever form fits your taste and schedule. I like to grate my garlic on a cheese grater rather than using a press, and I use real butter, which I melt in a pan and then brush onto the bread after the garlic has simmered. Some folks like just buttered bread. Some like to add Parmesan or some other cheese. Wrap the bread in foil and put it on a baking sheet, then bake at 400 degrees for 10 minutes or less.

Salad comes in a bag for anywhere from $1.69 to $2.00 and is easy to prepare, serve, and manage in its premixed form. However, it's almost as quick and more cost effective to blaze your own trail and make a tossed salad using lettuce (cleaned and torn rather than cut), tomatoes, carrots, and a bit of cucumber. Throw a few croutons on top, and your family will think you're a genius. Give them a Popsicle for dessert and you're a five-star chef.

By the way, while you are browning hamburger meat, you might want to brown an extra pound or so and store it for another meal. It'll come in handy later in the week for Sloppy Joes, soup, or taco meat.

Tuesday—Fish Sticks, French Fries, and Cooked Carrots

For this meal, you can use raw, frozen, or canned carrots. If you go with raw carrots, they'll need to be cleaned and cut, then steamed or boiled in your saucepan. Cook until the carrots reach the desired degree of softness. Drain, put some butter, salt, and pepper over them; a little brown sugar is also good for a change of pace. Then set them to the side or on a back burner set on low heat. The difference between the canned or frozen variety will be in the time it takes to soften. Fresh carrots take 20 to 40 minutes, depending on size and cut, so get on this first.

Heat 1 to 2 inches of vegetable oil or shortening in a deep pot on medium high to prepare for frying the French fries. (Frying is my favorite method—it's therapeutic for me—but baking is easier and less fatty if you prefer cooking them that way.) Meanwhile, preheat the oven and set your timer according to the instructions on the fish stick package. Place the sticks on a baking sheet, put them in the oven, and let them go.

While they cook, put a test French fry in the oil to see whether it's hot enough. If you get a rapid boiling sizzle, you should be good to go.

Watch to see if the fries brown too fast. If they brown quickly but don't cook through, your oil is too hot. Fry a batch, giving them long enough in the oil that they brown to golden and rise to the top of the oil. Also, the moisture boiling out should make the sizzle subside. Scoop them out and drain on a paper towel. If you are avoiding fats and looking for a leaner, easier way to prep, the fries can be baked, according to directions, using a cookie sheet.

When the fish is done you can serve it all up. If you want, salad or bread is always a nice complement. Macaroni and cheese can be substituted for the fries. Feel free to substitute peas or broccoli or corn for the carrots. Keep it simple and you won't go wrong.

Wednesday—Thank God for Hot Dogs!

Boil some hot dogs. Place them in self-serve mode on the stove. Heat some chili or Sloppy Joe sauce in a pan next to the dogs or in the microwave. Put out some buns, grated cheese, relish, other condiments, and fruit slices. If you want, slam some chips down on the counter and sit back while the kids chow down.

Thursday—Taco Salad

If you browned the hamburger on Monday, you're ahead of the game. If not, do it now. Drain and season with a package of taco seasoning or seasoned salt. Set it aside.

Make a salad. Crush some tortilla chips and sprinkle liberally over the salad in a large bowl. Add a can of kidney beans or pinto beans and a can of corn. Add the meat. Top with Catalina dressing, ranch dressing, or picante sauce. C'mon, it can't be this easy. But it is. The secret is in the knowing.

Friday—You Made It!

I usually make this day a get-what-you-can day since my kids are going in different directions. Heating up leftovers is a good choice for Friday dinner.

Saturday and Sunday

On weekends, I usually grill something. Hamburgers are a favorite, so I make plenty while I'm at it. Extras can be frozen and reheated in the microwave. They're also ideal for putting in the kids' lunches. If I grill chicken on Saturday, we eat it again on Sunday. This is a healthy, low-fat meat and serves to offset the beef we've been eating.

OTHER IDEAS

Here are a handful of other main course ideas, along with tasty side dish suggestions.

Stuffed Steak

Round steak is often on sale, so here are two easy ways to cook it: on the stove or in the slow cooker. You could also bake it.

Pound the round steak out to between one-half-inch and one-quarter-inch thick. Slice some garlic, onions, bell pepper, and carrots. Cut the round steak in half lengthwise. Place the sliced ingredients and a few cabbage leaves on the steak. Roll the steak and either tie it or close it with a toothpick.

In a large pot or pan with a lid, brown the steak rolls. Salt and pepper the outside while browning. Add one jar of spaghetti sauce and some water. Put the lid on and simmer on low heat for about 3 hours or until tender. If you cook rapidly on a higher heat, they will be done in an hour, but your flavors won't marry well. The slower you cook the steak, the more flavorful it will be.

If you use a slow cooker instead, set it on low and put the steak rolls, spaghetti sauce, and water in to simmer before you leave for work in the morning. They will be done by evening.

Serve with pasta, salad, and bread.

Easy Baked Potato

You can bake the potatoes in the oven or microwave—either when you plan to eat them or ahead of time. For example, if you're hanging around on Saturday, rinse some large russet potatoes. Take a fork and poke each potato a few times. Set the oven on 400 degrees and put the potatoes in for about 1 hour 15 minutes or until soft.

You can store them and reheat in the microwave when you're ready to eat. They make great after-school snacks or meals. Serve them with butter, sour cream, cheese, or any other desired toppings. We build a meal on top of baked potatoes by piling on chili, cheese, gravy, and/or crumbled bacon.

Rice

Place three cups of water to two cups of rice in a saucepan or pot that has a lid. Boil the water and rice uncovered on high until the water has cooked down to the level of the rice. Remove the pan from the heat and cover for 10 minutes. Perfect rice should be waiting.

You might want to rinse the rice before cooking until you get no more starchy whiteness coming off in the water. This gives you fluffy rice but washes away some of the nourishment. (Bonus tip: Brown or long-grain rice is more nourishing than white rice.) If you are doubling the recipe or if your stove burner cooks very hot or your pot is thin aluminum, stir the rice a little as it comes to a boil or while boiling. This will eliminate sticking and scorching.

Chicken

Boneless chicken breast isn't cheap, but it's a good value when you buy it in large quantities. You can microwave frozen breasts with lemon pepper or sprinkled with powdered ranch dressing mix. You can also marinate them in Italian dressing and toss them on the barbecue grill. Either way, it makes a healthy, tasty entrée.

Recipes á la Tracy[3]

Chicken and Rice-A-Roni

Lay four chicken breasts in the bottom of a baking dish. Pour a box of Rice-A-Roni into a large frying pan and brown in a little oil. Add the water and seasoning packet. Instead of simmering according to the directions on the box, pour the entire mixture over the chicken and bake at 350 degrees for 30 minutes.

Texas Pie

Brown hamburger meat and drain off the grease. In another pot make some instant mashed potatoes or boil and mash a few fresh potatoes. Mix the hamburger and the potatoes in a baking dish and top with cheese. Bake until the cheese is melted and the mixture is heated throughout.

Easy Enchiladas

Roll flour tortillas filled with grated cheese and place side by side in a baking dish. Pour one can of chili and one can of enchilada sauce over the filled tortillas. Top with chopped onions and grated cheese. Bake at 350 degrees for 20 minutes. For variety, fill the tortillas with a pasteurized cheese like Velveeta and top with Monterey Jack or mild cheddar. Any variation of the cheese will give you a unique taste. Another possibility for the filling is cream cheese and chicken. Top this with enchilada sauce and sour cream.

Simple-Fix Chicken and Dumplings

In a large pot, boil four or five chicken breasts until cooked through (20 to 30 minutes). Remove chicken and leave the water in the large pot. Cube the chicken and set to the side. Add two cans of cream of chicken soup to the water in which you boiled the chicken and return to boil. Open three tubes of cheap biscuits and separate the biscuits. Cut the biscuits into fourths. Drop into the boiling water and cook at a slow boil until they resemble dumplings and are cooked through (about 12 minutes). Add the chicken back into the broth mixture and simmer for 5 minutes. Salt and pepper to taste.

The kitchen is not as intimidating a place as it might seem. It's also a place that can be fun and provide a sense of accomplishment if you remember to be patient. Experiment when you can. Celebrate your successes and laugh at your failures. Occasionally, you're bound to oversalt or otherwise destroy a decent meal. Don't worry about it. If we can suck down soda pop from a convenience store at $1.00 a cup without blinking, unintentional waste in the kitchen shouldn't be the end of the world. Besides, if you're saving money and providing good fuel on a regular basis, hitting the fast-food fallback in case of disaster will be a welcome change rather than a regular drudge.

Survival Tips

Essential Kitchen Tools

One year for my birthday, when I was asked what gift I wanted, I said "salad tongs." No matter who asked, my reply was the same. When my birthday came and went, I was in tong heaven. I had plastic, metal, and wooden tongs. Years later I requested barbecue mops (a small mop for basting barbeque). You never know when you'll need more sauce on that grilled chicken. Both items are quite a source of laughter in our home. But remember: Get what you need. It's *your* toolbox for *your* kitchen.

Here's a list of tools, equipment, and cookware that will adequately outfit most kitchens:

- two small saucepans with lids
- one medium pot with lid
- one large stockpot with lid
- at least two frying pans. I use one small pan for eggs and light, quick cooking and a larger cast-iron skillet for larger, longer-cooking needs.
- large Dutch oven with a cast-iron lid (there are great deals on cast iron in many army surplus stores) or a covered Pyrex casserole dish. An alternative is to use disposable aluminum baking dishes for anything from casseroles to turkeys. Don't invest in a Dutch oven unless you will use it often.
- two baking sheets, for biscuits and cookies (one large enough to hold a big frozen pizza)

(continued)

- large baking pan or disposable aluminum baking dishes
- utensils: spatula, large spoon, wooden spoons, slotted spoons, serving fork, good knives in assorted sizes, tongs, melon baller, and pizza cutter
- miscellaneous: colander, large cutting board, can opener, blender, cheese grater, garlic press, deep fryer, storage containers, electric slow cooker

You can find these items at a discount store. Don't spend extra money on specialty items unless you're sure you'll use them. For instance, I like using a wok and oriental steamer, especially in the summer months when I do lighter meals with fewer carbs. I enjoy cooking, so such a purchase is worth it to me. There are also woks styled for the outdoor grill, great for grilling vegetables during warm-weather months.

Also, I have a collection of toasters. I'm tempted to use them as decorative ornaments in my yard. But, for the kitchen, one toaster is plenty.

10

THE WINDING PATH OF FAITH

God Hasn't Changed. He Still Loves Us.

SINCE WE'RE GOING to talk candidly about God, faith, spirituality, and grace in this chapter, I suppose I should come clean at the outset and make a confession: It's not easy for me to try to give you advice on how to practice the life of faith as a single dad.

It's not that I'm reluctant to talk about God and the life of faith. I am committed to God and his Son, and I'm a thankful, undeserving recipient of God's grace. I could talk about these things for hours. But here's where my reluctance comes in: Divorced dads and the children of divorce are sometimes hurt by religious people, so it can be hard for us to separate out the truth about God from the inappropriate words and actions of those who claim to know him. My children and I experienced some of this hurt. But we still love God with a desperate love. Our need for him and his strength and grace is a constant in our lives. And every day, we try to follow his Son as faithfully as we can. In other words, we remain committed Christians.

In this final chapter I don't want to talk about religion. Instead, I'd like to talk about how God wants to draw alongside you in the midst of the difficulty of raising your kids well as a single dad. For me, the life of faith can be summed up in one word: *relationship.* It's a relationship with God through his Son and a relationship with other people. I hope you'll find something of value in my story—even something of eternal value, a touch from God that will open your eyes in new ways to his love and the sacrifice his Son made for you and your children, and for all of us.

Faith is a challenge for everyone. Christian or free thinker, it doesn't matter. Faith poses a dilemma because believing in *anything*—whether it's gravity or a higher being—requires a leap into the unknown. You can see clear evidence of gravity all around you, just as you can observe evidence of the existence of God. But you can't *see* gravity any more than you can see God. Faith demands that we put our confidence in something invisible. And when it comes to believing in God, things get even more complicated. We have to confront questions about God and his involvement in the world that reach to the heart of our hurt and our human loss. For instance: If God *really* loved us, would he have allowed our marriages to fall apart?

The quick answer to that is yes, God still loves us no matter what happens in life. Pain and suffering in life are not evidence that God has turned his back on us. As for the dissolution of a marriage, God can't be held responsible. He created marriage to be a lifelong covenant.[1] Every marriage has three responsible parties, and two of them are humans. God can't force spouses to make their marriage survive.

So rather than get bogged down in a philosophical discussion about God and the problem of evil in the world, let's take a more personal look at God and our own lives as single dads. We'll start with life in general and then work our way back to God specifically.

ALL OF LIFE IS SPIRITUAL

I don't approach life as a dichotomy of religious and secular. I don't think of my work as strictly secular and my church involvement as solely religious. I don't have part of my life dedicated to God, part dedicated to my family, and part dedicated to myself. They are all one. All life comes forth from God and exists within that domain.

As a dad to my kids, I don't tend to their spiritual lives on certain days and the rest of their concerns the remainder of the time. I just take care of their lives. My guide is the Bible, and my view of God is that he is our Father and the Author of life. So when it comes to guiding my children through life, including the confusing and painful issues of divorce and broken families, I don't guide them spiritually with regard to some issues and nonspiritually with regard to others. I just guide them while remaining true to the principles on which I have built my own life. And those principles are derived from the truth of Scripture.

My children grew up attending church with a father who was, during many of those years, a pastor and missionary. My children often heard divorce spoken of as being "outside of God's desire for our lives." They had been promised that it would never happen to our family. They had been taught to let God's ways, as expressed in the Bible, be their ways—to live their lives by a higher standard, which means not giving in to destructive physical desires and emotional whims. They had been taught to believe that God loved them and was deeply interested in every detail of their lives. They had been taught the value of independent thinking and interdependent living. And they had been taught that the greatest gift of God is his grace freely given to undeserving humans, as evidenced in the saving sacrifice of his Son.

Then my wife left, and many of my children's hopes and dreams—as well as their illusions of their parents—were called into question. At that time, the only thing I taught them that mattered was grace. If I had been a narrow religious dad who had raised my kids to focus on following rules more than to loving God, it would have been easy for my children to become self-righteous accusers. If I had been inconsistent or wishy-washy in my convictions, it would have been easy for my children to shrug off all they knew about giving their lives to Christ and instead do whatever they wanted.

If I hadn't been honest and trustworthy in the past, it would have been easy for my children to assume the worst about their parents and conclude that they might as well discard the faith their parents had taught them. Both their mother and I had broken a promise to love and cherish each other for life, and our children understandably questioned why we had chosen to separate. My kids mourned, but they didn't lose hope.

First Corinthians 13:5 says that love keeps no record of wrongs. My ex-wife and I would need the forgiving love and grace of our children to pull us through; our kids would need love to pull themselves through. Amid all the pain and anger and sorrow and damaged self-image, forgiveness is key. In fact, it might be *the* key not only to survival but to recovery.

BUILD A SPIRITUAL FOUNDATION

Whatever your past, no matter how angry your kids are and no matter how badly you have messed up, start building a tradition of integrity in your convictions. Model it for your children. Teach them. Without a foundation in something solid, you and your children have nothing to support you in the storms of life. Everything I was able to do for my children in terms of spiritual guidance during and after divorce was because of what I had done *before* the divorce.

Were the foundations shaken? Like never before. Did they survive? You bet your life they did.

The biggest thing I did during and after my divorce was the same thing I did before. I modeled love, grace, and self-discipline as best I could. I confessed my failings. I loved my children and modeled love for their mother despite my hurt and anger. I pushed myself to spend meaningful time in fellowship and in worshiping God with others who shared my Christian faith. I continued to pray and study the Bible, even when I wanted to give up hope, even when I was furious with God for not rescuing my family. I continued to work out my own salvation with fear and trembling in light of God's grace as best I could.[2]

Jesus teaches that righteousness begins and ends within. It's not what is outside a person that corrupts him, but what is inside him that shows who that person really is.[3] Righteous and just behavior is found in a person who is actively and consistently pursuing the removal of logs that blind his own eyes rather than looking for the faults of others.[4] Jesus teaches us to practice mercy toward others ahead of acts of religious devotion.[5] He teaches to love others with the same devotion with which we love ourselves.[6] He teaches a life of service to others instead of sclf-service.[7] Jesus teaches us to be healers, peacemakers, caretakers, bringers of justice, and lovers of God.

Do I feel strongly about my faith? I feel more strongly about my faith than anything in this world. And that is one reason my children survived this mess as well as they did.

A father is a teacher. If you don't teach your children, someone else will. The only way to ensure they are being taught well is for you to teach them. Certainly you must rely on the help of others, such as the school system and your church, but don't turn the responsibility completely over to others. From the time they are babies, teach your children the things they need to know about God and what it means to follow his Son. You don't have to be a biblical scholar; you just have to be an honest follower of Jesus yourself. Giving them instruction and living your life as a model of faith is your duty as a dad.

A father is also a priest. Make intercession for your family in prayer and do it every day. Teach your children how to pray and talk freely with God, pouring out all of their fears and questions and hurts and anger. Lay your hands on them and pray when they're sick. Remind them of the words and works of God. Speak to them of God's love and model it whenever you can.

A father is also a provider. Do the best you can to provide for your children's physical needs. Use all of your power and skills and abilities to serve them well.

A father is also a protector. Get involved in the lives of your children. Protect them by disciplining and defending them properly. Protect them by loving them and by being there for them. Listen to them and learn their needs.

In short, do the things God instructs you to do. The spiritual life is not about some whimsy you feel inside. It's about the powerful force and living presence of God, his indwelling Spirit who enables us to live properly for God. Follow God's commands, and when you fail, confess your sins to him. Then get back up and begin again to do the right things. Without this kind of foundation, the struggle to recover from divorce will be a losing battle. But love is patient, so begin where you are and don't lose heart.

CARING FOR YOUR KIDS DURING CRISIS

At the time of my separation I had four children ranging in age from six years to fifteen years. Each child was in a different stage of personal development, so each was in a different stage of spiritual development as well. I'd like to tell you a little about each of them:

Jennifer: A Determined Faith

Jennifer, my oldest, had been attending church for several years as the daughter of a pastor, missionary, and Bible teacher. She had attended two different Christian schools. She had been home-schooled, primarily using curriculum with a Christian worldview. She was very knowledgeable about the Bible. She was also very independent, smart, and perceptive. She was inquisitive and questioning. She was logical.

Jennifer had fallen away from church attendance before her mother and I separated. She was being labeled as rebellious by a religious crowd that didn't understand her actions and her choices in fashion and physical appearance. However, I knew her and trusted her. Therefore it was easy to give her room to be herself. I had no reason to panic. Jennifer had some friends whose behavior was suspect, but I knew that she knew where the boundaries were. Besides, at fifteen, if a teenage child won't exercise self-control based upon her personal commitment to follow

God, a parent can't make much difference. You can advise. You can steer with wisdom. If you try to control, though, you will likely fail. And the failure may not be evident for many years.

I let Jennifer know that despite the failings of her parents, God would never desert her. I reminded her that it is only by grace that each of us receives favor with God. I encouraged her not to forsake her personal relationship with God. I prayed with her whenever I had the opportunity, without demanding that she pray out loud or that she pray at all. I asked occasionally if she was reading Scripture, and regardless of her answer I didn't judge her. She knew her responsibilities, and any conviction necessary would be supplied by God's Spirit. My job was to lead and encourage.

I was present as well for damage control. I was there to help pick up the pieces if she crashed and burned. I was there to nudge her out of the nest at the proper time and to see that she was prepared when that time came. I was not there to force her to adhere to my views or else hit the road.

I've watched too many parents resort to fear tactics to control their children. Today my daughter works for an attorney and is paying her way through college. She has a good relationship with God. Her failures have been minimal and her recovery speedy. Many of her friends who grew up in more pristine and controlling environments are still struggling to find the right path in life. Some are substance abusers, sexually promiscuous, and hiding their private lives from their parents. Some of those children, now young adults, still come to me for help because their relationship with their parents is broken and empty.

A teenager only submits to authority willingly when he or she believes and respects the authority figure. If you want your children to walk along a path with you, teach them that you love them, and do what you can to earn their trust. Trust is built by a consistent life that supports what you've been teaching.

Ian: A Quiet Faith

Ian, my older son, is another story. His faith is very dear and is kept personal. He prays best quietly, alone in his room. He likes an ordered church service. He is comfortable in a well-disciplined, controlled environment. Whereas Jennifer likes a looser, contemporary worship setting, Ian wants tradition.

Ian attends church with his friends. He needs the crowd in part for insulation and affirmation and in part just because he's social. I encourage him to remain faithful in prayer. I ask occasionally if he is reading Scripture. Sometimes I ask his opinion of a verse. I do this for two reasons. One, to hear his thoughts. Two, to let it serve as a reminder that I hold Scripture in the highest regard and am myself a student. In karate you learn that there are times for a full frontal attack, times for a subtle attack from the side or rear, and times for a quiet counterattack. Parenting, like fighting, requires thought, strategy, and a variety of methods.

I remind Ian of the importance of God by praying with him before sporting events. We thank God for Ian's talent and for his opportunity to utilize those talents. In all areas of life, we pray first whenever there is any type of crisis or difficult decision. This is a standard with all of the children. If a decision needs to be made, I listen, offer advice, then encourage the children to pray and take the night (or whatever time is appropriate) to listen for God's answer. When offering my opinion, I give it as an opinion, not as law. I always encourage them to leave room for their thoughts and their sense of what God is saying to them. If they think God is saying something that differs from my advice, I let them hear from God. Whether their decision proves good or bad, they are learning about discernment. Learning to make good decisions often is the result of learning hard lessons from earlier poor decisions.

Of course, there are always instances when something takes place that needs a dad's attention and requires that the child trust parental leadership. If one of my children had said that God told him to do something I deemed not in his best interest or out of keeping with godly instruction, then I would step in to teach, counsel, and pray that child back onto a sound path. Sometimes a child must trust that her parent is hearing from God *for* her. But remember, kids will only trust the parent if the foundation for trust has already been laid by the parent's consistent life.

Paige: A Wounded Faith

Paige's situation was the photo negative of Ian and Jennifer. Whereas Jennifer and Ian had a typical level of church involvement for teenagers, my younger daughter practically *lived* at church. God was on her sleeve, and her testimony was ever on her lips.

Paige believed God would rescue her family from divorce. A well-meaning woman in our church who was mentoring Paige said that if she had faith and prayed the rest of us back into a "proper" relationship with God, he would restore our family. She was told that her family was disobedient and far from God. Paige was taught a skewed interpretation of Scripture. Verses from the Bible were taken out of context or over-literalized. She lived in fear and the belief that her family members were in danger of certain destruction. She felt guilty and ashamed of her family. And she was afraid of the judgment of her peers and her mentor. To this day the girls who are part of that church's fellowship are encouraged not to socialize with Paige but, instead, to pray for her and her family.

The problems that this type of teaching produced were substantially different from the problems I experienced with my other children. And today, while the others have rebounded well, Paige continues to suffer from hurt and distrust of church people.

I didn't want to appear defensive. Yet, as the one charged with her spiritual well-being, I knew I needed to take an active approach in correcting her path.

I fell back on a tried-and-true approach that had worked in my own life. I decided to let the proper teaching of Scripture speak for itself. The power of the Word of God is immeasurable. I had seen this work in the lives of others when I was a pastor and Bible teacher. So when Paige would mention something that reflected what she was being taught, I would ask her to show me in the Bible where the teaching had come from. Then I would have her read it in context and tell me what she thought it really meant. I would also have her look up verses that supported proper interpretation, verses that held up in light of the Bible's overall message. I would ask her what she thought, and I'd ask her to pray for clarity and understanding. She began to discover the cracks in the teaching she was receiving.

Today, she continues to pray and read Scripture. In time she will heal, though she is still hurt by the friends who turned their backs on her. I love her and remind her not to run from God. I pray for her healing, both in private and when we are praying together. I am trying to model forgiveness, though it's tough for me to be tolerant of people who are more concerned about personal agendas than the complete truth of God.

Jesus teaches us to love our enemies and pray for them.[8] He commanded it, so I try to obey.

THE WINDING PATH OF FAITH

Nico: An Emerging Faith

And then there is Nico. When his mother left, Nico, who was not yet six, was impressionable and vulnerable and not very well anchored in Christian faith. I prayed and taught him quietly while looking for good fellowship for him as a small boy. God provided the perfect vehicle.

Nico loves a good show. He always has. I was the director of a theater when Nico was five, six, and seven years old. I've been a performer for as long as Nico can remember. He loves the costumes, the lights, and the production.

A Christian theater troupe came to town with a show that was bigger than life. It had lightning, fire, smoke, sound, heaven, and hell. Angels and Satan himself made appearances. To me, the show was hype and melodrama. To Nico, it was a vision of the truth. He stepped forward to entrust his life to Christ in response to an invitation offered at the end of the production.

For those youngsters who made a profession of faith, there was a program in which elder citizens had volunteered to meet with the children and teach them a simple Bible study designed to answer their questions and root them in the Christian faith. Nico's name was spotted by an elderly woman who knew our family through her granddaughter, who had taken gymnastics with Jennifer. This lady offered to meet with Nico and another young boy. She was a gracious woman, very patient and loving. For Nico, whose mother had just moved to another city, the weekly trips to "Grandmother's" house for cookies, fellowship, and Bible study were nothing short of a miraculous gift from God.

Praise God I don't parent alone, even as a single dad. I could never have devised such a wonderful plan for meeting Nico's spiritual needs in the midst of family crisis.

And here is a truth. I committed my children back to their Maker at their birth. I can't raise them. I don't even manage my own life as well as I should. God raises my children. Sometimes he raises them through me, sometimes despite me. When I talk to God, I remind him that my children are his and that I need him to make me a fitting steward of the young lives he has entrusted to me.

Part of what keeps me going as a single dad is the love and care of other Christians. I teach a Bible study at a dinner group attended by folks who have been hurt by the institutional church but still love God. We meet in homes and study the Scriptures and worship God together. We support one another in Christian love, and we support other Christian ministries. Last month our group sent two missionaries to Cuba to do short-term mission work. We gave twenty turkeys to the Salvation Army at Thanksgiving. We are a small church without a church building—much like the first churches described in the book of Acts. We gather regularly for fellowship, study, and prayer.

All of us need the support of others who love and follow God. If a formal church setting works for you, by all means take that route. There are many traditional churches that understand the needs of single parents and do a great job of reaching out. But if a formal church doesn't appeal to you, don't give up on Christian fellowship. Find another group of believers you can join. We *all* need to spend regular, meaningful time in fellowship with other Christians.

A LOOK AT YOUR OWN SITUATION

Some of you are saying, "Well, sure, this fits *your* circumstances. But my situation is far different. My wife is antagonistic toward Christianity, and she has the kids more than I do. What am I supposed to do when she tells the kids I'm a religious nut?"

To arrive at an answer, let me take you on a short trip with Chaplain Klumpp. For several years I was a chaplain and religious program director in a privately managed prison facility. I'd been working in ministry on the streets with the same type of guys. Now I was working with them on the other side of the prison wall.

One big difference in a prison setting was that by law I was required to meet the spiritual needs of persons of *any* faith. With so many religions represented, I had trouble understanding how I could remain true to my own convictions and still properly assist every inmate who came to me for pastoral assistance. What do you do when you're a Christian and someone tells you he needs a menorah or tarot cards to practice his religion?

Most chaplains either take the easy road and let such requests fall on deaf ears, telling inmates they'll have to talk to someone else about arranging what was requested. I believed I was in the position of chaplain through God's leadership and direction, so I decided to seek God's advice on how to handle inmates with faiths that differ from my own. Understand that this is a serious issue, going far beyond considerations of religious freedom. Some religious organizations in prison are hardly more than gangs. Also, many inmates test the system by making outrageous requests, hoping that the requests will be denied, thus giving the inmate an opportunity to sue the system. I didn't have time for lawsuits and only wanted to do the right thing.

According to government regulation, each inmate had a right to practice his religion. And according to our setup, as the chaplain I was the go-to guy on religious matters. So I prayed.

God reminded me of my work on the streets. He then proceeded to emphasize some verses of Scripture: "Greater love has no one than this, that he lay down his life for his friends."[9] "By this all men will know that you are my disciples, if you love one another."[10] "Love your neighbor as yourself."[11] "Do to others as you would have them do to you."[12] "Love your enemies and pray for those who persecute you."[13] And so on.

To me, the teachings of Jesus meant that I could never truly love an inmate who adhered to another religion while insisting that he first convert to Christianity. Nor could I love him while ignoring his request for pastoral assistance. Paul reasoned with the pagan philosophers in ancient Athens without condemning their error but, instead, by appealing to their hunger for higher knowledge.[14] Paul found a small bit of common ground with these philosophers, and he used that to begin a conversation about the one true God. So I chose to love the inmates by helping them if I could. I didn't worship with those who didn't practice Christianity, since their beliefs conflicted with my own. But neither did I inhibit their worship. Then I turned my efforts over to God, in prayer, asking him to somehow use the spiritual hunger in these inmates to turn their hearts toward his truth.

Still, I wasn't sure I was doing enough to guide the men toward God. Over time, this is what I saw.

I assisted the Muslim inmates in having the local imam come to the jail. I helped the Moorish Science inmates obtain literature on their religion. I contacted a rabbi and asked him to bring a menorah and tarot cards to the inmate I mentioned earlier. (For some reason, this man wanted both of these items, even though tarot cards have nothing to do with Judaism.) The rabbi declined the request, by the way.

The more I assisted the inmates, all the while answering their questions about my own faith, the more I saw inmates joining me in Bible study and worship services to the true God. "Klumpp," they would say, "no one ever did anything like this for us before. I want to know your Jesus." I laid the bricks of love. God built the bridge.

So if your ex-wife is leading your children in a spiritual direction that contradicts your Christian beliefs, take a risk. Lead without words. By that I mean don't get caught in battles or locked into strident positions that pit you against her. If you feel you have to address an issue directly, do it with gentle words and with Scripture. Don't be angry or judgmental. Keep to the issues. Teach and model. Don't get caught tearing down or shaming the competition. Instead, sell your strengths. Emphasize the value and validity of Christian faith. Let God's truth speak for itself.

Then make sure you are consistently living out your faith in daily life. Love God, love your kids, love your ex-wife. (Yes, even if she's wiccan.) Remember, Jesus teaches us to pray for our enemies and to do good to those who mistreat us.[15] Use your life to teach your kids about God's love, and add your gentle words to teach them whenever they're in your care. Demonstrate your faith in pure action, and then pray, pray, pray. Don't turn spiritual practice into harsh confrontation, but instead commit your children and their spiritual welfare to God. And trust him with the outcome. Model God's love, not legalistic religion.

MAKING IT PERSONAL

So that's my story, at least the part that matters here. Some of it might fit your own story, and much may differ. One thing is certain though: We all struggle and the struggle continues. But while we struggle, God promises that those who honestly seek him will eventually find him.[16] In your struggles, always be mindful of that promise.

You may be tempted to give up on God. I remember choosing one Sunday to go before my congregation to confess all the sin and failings that led to the demise of my marriage. Anticipating sympathy, I received rejection instead. I had admitted my own wrongdoing, which made me the odd man out. I left the church angry and confused. I didn't mind God so much as the people he seemed to hang out with. My faith was being tested as never before. Somehow, by God's grace, I managed to hold onto God while reassessing the practices of some of his followers.

Be honest in your struggles. It doesn't help anything to try to hide doubts or questions or disillusionment from God. He can take it, so go ahead and dish it out. Tell him everything and then listen to what he has to say to you.

Hang tough, no matter the hurt, opposition, or confusion. Your honest search for God and his truth will spill over into the lives of your children as you begin to encounter God on your own. Your children are watching and waiting for help for their own hurts. If God is real and his Word is true, then he has not left you or forsaken you.[17]

If your ex is antagonistic toward your faith, if she seems to be shielding your kids from your "self-righteous mythology," as my faith has been labeled, don't lose your cool. Knee-jerk reactions generally just fuel the fires against us. Be patient. Trust God. Love your ex and pray for her and your kids. These are times not only to get radical in your faith, but also to get real. Be real in pursuing the truth of Christ. "Be imitators of God, therefore, as dearly loved children."[18]

Then again, maybe you're not reading this book to get advice about following God. Fair enough. I hope the strategies and the practical suggestions in the previous chapters will help you achieve success as a single dad. But if you're hurting just like the rest of us and wondering if there isn't more to life than what you see in the physical world, why not issue God a challenge? In doing so, you're really not risking anything. If he's not there, you'll lose nothing. So for a moment, if you choose, suspend your disbelief and open your mind and heart to the possibilities. What

I offer is the living God who cares about you and who will come to your aid. Perhaps not in ways you expect, but he will not ignore you.

The energy it takes to ask God to reveal himself is a small step toward encountering the God of the universe, the One who entered our world in the form of a man and who suffered all the indignity and abuse and scorn and rejection possible for one man to endure.[19] That's the God who knows your heart, your pain, your anger, your bitterness, and your doubt. Talk to that God. Pour out your heart to him. Ask him to open your eyes and heart to his presence, his love, and his desire to heal the hurts you and your children are experiencing.

If that's where you are today, and you're willing to give God a chance, let me tell you what I did when I was in your shoes. One night in 1979, after years of searching for spiritual reality and not finding it, I said, "Listen, God, I don't know who you are or what you are. But if you reveal yourself to me, I will follow you." I believe God honored those words and the genuineness of my heart's desire. During my divorce and the time following, I have prayed, "God, there's a lot going on that I don't understand. Please help me see you. Please help my kids. Please let us know you're there." If you want to, borrow my words or my sentiment and reach out to God. He will not fail you.

Living out your faith is not the discipline of abiding by a set of religious rules; it's a sometimes messy, day-to-day journey of seeking God's face and then seeking to obey him. As I mentioned at the beginning of this chapter, life is not compartmentalized. God figures into *all* of life, not just the occasional "religious activity."

My family has remained faithful to God through a wrenching crisis, with progress and setbacks, and through difficult questions and struggles. I pray that you and your children, against your own backdrop of brokenness, will know this same healing touch of God. He is the only One who knows us better than we know ourselves. In his mercy and grace, he desires to make something beautiful from the broken pieces of our lives.

Remember, God loves us and he never fails us.

Survival Tips

Thoughts for a Warrior's Spirit

- A man who wants nothing has everything.
- What good is it to be a warrior if you don't know what is worth fighting for?
- A true warrior is not independent but interdependent.
- Leading means going first.

Verses for a Weary Spirit

- "Come to me, all you who are weary and burdened, and I will give you rest" (Matthew 11:28).
- "The LORD is my light and my salvation—whom shall I fear?" (Psalm 27:1).
- "In all these things we are more than conquerors through him who loved us" (Romans 8:37).
- "God made you alive with Christ. He forgave us all our sins" (Colossians 2:13).
- "Be strong and courageous. Do not be afraid or terrified because of them, for the LORD your God goes with you; he will never leave you nor forsake you" (Deuteronomy 31:6).

Introduction

1. I raised my four kids as the primary caregiver in joint custody for several years. My children were ages six through fifteen when I was divorced. I am now remarried and pleased to be the father and stepfather of eight children.

Chapter 1

1. If your ex-wife was habitually abusive or chronically unfaithful, divorce can bring a sense of relief. The hope of a good outcome and a lasting marriage may have died long before the divorce was final. Still, a lifelong bond is what we all hope for when we first commit to marriage.

2. It's good to do everything you can to work on your own faults in an effort to try to win back the one you love. It's possible that your good-faith efforts will carry the day. Yet beware of obsessing. Recognize that your efforts can't guarantee success.

3. See 2 Corinthians 12:9.

4. For the details of this story, see 2 Samuel 12:15-23. To read the prayer of confession that David uttered after his acts of adultery and conspiracy to commit murder, see Psalm 51.

5. See Ecclesiastes 3:1-8.

6. See Matthew 7:3-5.

7. This famous quote is traditionally attributed to Vince Lombardi. For more quotes on fatigue, visit www.quoteme onit.com/fatigue.html.

8. Hebrews 12:11.

Chapter 2

1. John 15:13.

2. See Genesis 1:26-27.

3. See Romans 8:31.

Chapter 3

1. See Genesis 2:15-17 and Genesis 3. Even Adam and Eve had a choice in how they would respond to God.

2. See Hebrews 12:7-11.

3. The way my daughter was treated at church was another matter, however. A few families there continued to insist that Jennifer was a rebel. This so wounded my daughter's spirit that she dropped out of church and is still struggling with going back. She loves God, but the killing nature of legalism did the work of turning her off of church.

4. See Genesis 3:11-13.

5. Some dads may have anger problems or were themselves victims of abusive discipline when they were children. These individuals may need to set different restraints on their actions. Often, counseling will be helpful. Don't be embarrassed to seek help. Your children's welfare is at risk. If you have any doubts in this matter, ask someone you trust for his input.

6. John Prine, *A John Prine Christmas* (Oh Boy Records, 1993), compact disc, track 2.
7. Genesis 2:9.

Chapter 4

1. See Proverbs 31:30; Genesis 1:27; Psalm 139:13-16.
2. Proverbs 22:6.
3. A good source for such a certificate—and other great advice on remaining sexually abstinent and biblically pure—is www.truelovewaits.com.

Chapter 5

1. Robert Frost, "Mending Wall," *The Poetry of Robert Frost,* ed. Edward Connery Lathem (New York: Henry Holt, 1979), 33.
2. I will forever be indebted to John Bill's mother for her compassion and care for my younger son.
3. Go to www.mannersbymichele.com for useful information on all aspects of table manners. Also, if you input the word *etiquette* in your search engine, it will provide you with various sites on etiquette for every occasion, from a golf date to the proper care and respect for the nation's flag.

Chapter 6

1. Jesus defines this type of sacrifice for another person as the greatest love. He said, "Greater love has no one than this, that he lay down his life for his friends" (John 15:13).
2. Proverbs 24:33-34.

3. Philippians 4:13, NASB.

4. Joshua 1:9.

5. For the computer-oriented person, this same system can easily be set up on spreadsheets. It can also be done with a preprinted personal organizer, readily available at any office supply store.

Chapter 7

1. Herman Melville, *Moby Dick* (New York: Barnes & Noble, 1993), 478.

2. See Ecclesiastes 3:12-13,22.

3. See Mark 12:28-31.

4. See Luke 10:38-42.

Chapter 8

1. See Psalm 18:19; 147:11.

2. See Hebrews 12:7-12.

3. Statistic on personality development noted during class lectures on pastoral psychology, presented by Frank Minirth and Paul Meier at Dallas Theological Seminary, Spring 1985, Dallas, Texas.

4. See Psalm 127:5.

5. See 2 Corinthians 6:4-10; Philippians 4:11-12.

6. Psalm 46:10.

7. Psalm 46:10, NASB.

8. See Genesis 1:26-27.

9. On God's creation of humankind, see Genesis 1:27; 2:4-25. On being wonderfully made, see Psalm 139:14. On being bought with a price, see 1 Corinthians 6:20; 7:23. On

God's promise to never leave us, see Deuteronomy 31:6; Hebrews 13:5. On viewing our children as a gift from God, see Psalm 127. On ambition being nothing more than empty striving, see Ecclesiastes 2:11,17. On loving yourself and others, see Matthew 22:39; Galatians 5:14. On God's incredible love for us, see John 3:16.

10. On reflecting God's love by loving others, see John 13:34-35.
11. On setting your children as your first priority in loving and serving others, see 1 Timothy 3:4-5,12-13; 5:8; Titus 1:6.

Chapter 9

1. See Genesis 25:29-34.
2. See John 21:4-12.
3. The final four recipes come from a friend and single mom who sent me some great meal-planning ideas. Her recipes are tasty and easy to prepare. Thanks, Tracy.

Chapter 10

1. See Genesis 2:20-24; Malachi 2:16; Matthew 19:4-6.
2. See Philippians 2:12.
3. See Mark 7:14-15,20-23.
4. See Matthew 7:3-5.
5. See Matthew 12:7; Hosea 6:6.
6. See Luke 6:31; Matthew 19:19; Leviticus 19:18.
7. See Matthew 23:11-12.
8. See Matthew 5:44.
9. John 15:13.
10. John 13:35.
11. Matthew 19:19.

12. Luke 6:31.
13. Matthew 5:44.
14. See Acts 17:16-34.
15. See Matthew 5:44.
16. See Jeremiah 29:11-14.
17. See Deuteronomy 31:6.
18. Ephesians 5:1.
19. See Matthew 27:27-31,46.